D1546442

GEORGE GISSING: THE CULTURAL CHALLENGE

George Gissing: The Cultural Challenge

JOHN SLOAN
Lecturer in English
Balliol College, Oxford

St. Martin's Press   New York

First published in the United States of America in 1989

Printed in the Peoples' Republic of China

ISBN 0–312–02409–6

Library of Congress Cataloging-in-Publication Data
Sloan, John, 1948–
    George Gissing: the cultural challenge / by John Sloan.
        p.   cm.
    Bibliography: p.
    Includes index.
    ISBN 0–312–02409–6: $35.00 (est.)
    1. Gissing, George, 1857–1903—Criticism and interpretation.
I. Title
PR4717.S55   1989
823'.3—dc19   88–18815
                                                         CIP

For my father and mother
Joseph and Sheila Sloan

Contents

Contents

Acknowledgements

I am indebted to a number of scholars in the field of Gissing studies, notably to Jacob Korg, whose *George Gissing: A Critical Biography* (1965) remains the best introduction to Gissing's life and work, and to Pierre Coustillas, for his pioneering scholarship. I should also like to acknowledge my debt to two critics who deeply influenced the direction of this study – to Adrian Poole, whose *Gissing in Context* (1975) promoted a new critical context within which the significance of Gissing's work could be discussed, and to John Goode, whose *George Gissing: Ideology and Fiction* (1978) marked an important critical and theoretical departure from his earlier, essentially 'Lukácsian' assessment of Gissing's work.

I am very grateful to Terry Eagleton for his advice and many kindnesses during the writing of the doctoral thesis which was the first form of the present study, and to Valentine Cunningham, John Goode and Bob White for their comments and criticisms. Finally I should like to thank Roger Lonsdale and Carl Schmidt, who welcomed me to Balliol College; Stefan Olafsson, for the gift of a very useful book; and my wife Elizabeth, who first suggested Gissing and who gave practical help and support at every stage of the work.

Parts of Chapters 2 and 7 have appeared previously in *The Gissing Newsletter* and *English Literature in Transition* and I thank the editors of these journals for permission to reprint this material.

J.S.

Introduction

*I fail as yet to make out why exactly it is that
going so far he so sturdily refuses to go further.*

Henry James

The view expressed by P. J. Keating over a decade ago – that 'few
writers of comparable stature can have been rediscovered so often
to so little effect as Gissing'[1] – would no longer seem to be true.
The revival of interest among scholars and critics has laid the basis
of a convincing alternative to the traditional view of Gissing as a
fascinating failure. A compelling aspect of this general process of
rediscovery has been the recognition not only of the centrality of
Gissing's novels, but of the challenging nature of their realisation
and effect. Yet although the particularity of Gissing's work is
now less likely to be conceived in narrowly personal terms,
his place continues to be that of a literary curiosity who stands
between two major periods of literary art. The characterisation
of Gissing's minor status in terms of the transitional nature of
his work partly reflects the response of present-day criticism
in general to the indigenous English novel of the *fin de siècle*,
and specifically to what is generally seen as the decline of the
English realist tradition into the naturalism of Gissing, Wells and
Bennett. It will be the purpose of this introduction to examine, in
an inevitably schematic form, Gissing's place in the intellectual,
cultural and literary framework of the late-Victorian period. The
intention, however, is not to promote the claims of Gissing's
centrality or place in that large-scale aesthetic disruption which
can be seen to transform the spirit and tenor of English literature
from the late 1850s on. Rather it is to provide a perspective from
which the continuing cultural challenge and disturbing artistic
significance of his work can be located. Similarly, the aim of this
study as a whole will not be to question Gissing's minor place
in the traditional literary canon, but rather to offer a reading of

1

his novels that will attempt to make visible something of their problematic relation to our received notions of literature, and specifically to the traditions of realism within which he writes.

It is in itself somewhat contradictory that the perceived limitations of Gissing's work are so often accepted as being a consequence of an ill-balanced nature when this imbalance is itself just as commonly located in the general conditions of his education and class. To relegate Gissing's repressive gentility and cherished antiquarianism to a merely private phenomenon is to overlook the crucial role played by family life and educational institutions in actively shaping individuals to the particular ends and expectations of a culture as a whole. The biographical details that follow are intended to delineate the wider social implications of Gissing's inner separation from the social realities of his times. The purpose is not in any direct way to question those earlier psychological interpretations of Gissing's life and work which have yielded their own valuable insights. Nor, however, is it to offer a more general frame of reference through which to connect Gissing's imaginative outlook in any representative sense with those of his contemporaries. The aim is to probe the real social and ideological tensions of that 'inner separation' or 'exile'. Gissing's case is particularly revealing in this respect since the very terms through which he seeks to express his sense of autonomy and independence of the society serve paradoxically to revoke all such claims to individual transcendence. It is a conflict which, as we shall see, enters with disturbing, alienating effects into the very structure of the novel form itself.

in general to the indigenous English novel of the mid-late period, and specifically to what is generally seen as the decline of the English realist tradition into the mannerism of Gissing, Wells and

It is a sign perhaps of Gissing's contemporaneity, as well as of our own unromantic view of lower middle-class life in general that the heroic, and sometimes dramatic history of Gissing and his family should finally be viewed in the kind of prosaic and familiar light which prevents admiration. Of his father, Thomas Waller Gissing, we know that he began life as the son and grandson of shoemakers in Halesworth, Suffolk, and that his brothers became drapers' assistants. Thomas Gissing trained as a pharmacist and held positions as a chemist's assistant before purchasing his own business in Wakefield in 1856. Much less is known of Gissing's mother, Margaret Bedford, who married Thomas Gissing in

Wordsworth's church in Grasmere in 1857, the year George Gissing was born. It has frequently been said of her that she was the daughter of a Droitwich solicitor, but recent research suggests that she may have had a more humble background.[2]

The conditions of Gissing's upbringing and family life would thus seem to be marked by exile in a double sense. The move to Wakefield, as Gillian Tindall has pointed out, represented a shift from rural community to mill town which was 'typical of the immediately post-Industrial Revolutionary wave of socio-geographical mobility'.[3] Their separation from family associations and past ties was not only the result of geographical accident or economic need; it became the condition of their deepest social and cultural aspirations. Though Thomas Gissing was agnostic and radical in sympathy, his involvement in the municipal politics of his adopted community reflects something of that effective political and cultural incorporation of lower-class ambition which was to characterise English society from the mid-nineteenth century onwards. His educational zeal as an executive member of the Wakefield Mechanics' Institution, and later Treasurer of the Liberal Party and Town Councillor, seems to have combined in his case with an aversion for 'the people'.[4]

It is significant that the lives of his children should have been marked by an insulation from local life.[5] The personal aspects of this segregation have perhaps been over-emphasised. Henry Hick, for instance, has left us a pen picture of the healthy gregariousness of Gissing as a boy.[6] The isolation of the Gissing children was to some degree characteristic of lower middle-class life as it was to develop in England in the nineteenth century. It was a condition perhaps necessary for those without entrance to society who sought nevertheless to dissociate themselves from the life of 'the masses'. The privacy of the Gissing household might be compared in some respects to that of the Brontës at Haworth; and indeed it is not surprising that the characteristic note of ambiguous withdrawal in Gissing's novels should have found an earlier expression in the works of Charlotte Brontë, a writer in whom Gissing himself was to acknowledge 'an intense personal interest'.[7]

Literature provided Gissing with an imaginative release from the evident repressions and isolation of life behind the chemist's shop. Gissing's father, according to H. G. Wells, was in this respect a 'cardinal formative influence in his life.'[8] Thomas Gissing had himself already published a small volume of poems before moving to Wakefield,[9] though these consist for the most part of conventional, rather stilted imitations of the 'Nature' poets. His interests – he was later the author of two small works on the ferns and flora of the local countryside[10] – would seem in an almost anachronistic way to display something of that combined attachment to poetry and natural science which had been characteristic of the temper of the dissenting academies in the previous century. It was later to puzzle Gissing that his father's evident literacy had co-existed with the ignorant belief that Greek and Latin poetry rhymed.[11]

The reason for this puzzlement lies in the fact that his own education was strangely 'traditional' by contrast. His classical training had already begun in the collegiate department of the local Artisan's School in Wakefield before he was thirteen. Visiting Rome in 1888, he was to write to his sister Margaret of 'places that have been familiar to one's imagination since Harrison's Back Lane School'.[12] Lindow Grove, the Quaker boarding school at Alderley Edge which Gissing and his two brothers attended after Thomas Gissing's death in 1870, was directed by the ideal of a classical education. The emphasis of the school curriculum on the effectiveness of Latin grammar in organising and training the mind[13] clearly reflects the influence of faculty psychology and the widespread nineteenth-century notion of 'mind-training' on the earlier Georgian ideals of classical learning.[14] The traditional aims of forming character and providing a basis of shared values and ideals were in fact preserved in the form of a Christian-humanist ethos propagated from the 1820s by educators such as Thomas Arnold. The boys at Alderley Edge were 'taught to be gentlemen, to have a hatred of all meanness, and insincerity, and a love of all things lovely, true, and of good report'.[15] Yet, according to Sheldon Rothblatt, the ethos of sociability in the nineteenth-century idea of a liberal education was revived not because 'of a new central core of social values', but for the 'same reason that mental training remained the dominant psychological learning theory of the nineteenth century'.[16] The attempt to harness the 'radical adventurousness' of an increasingly studious and educated population was characterized by the creation of a sub-culture, often founded upon the teacher's own personality or values, to replace the general culture; of this sub-culture, Rothblatt argues, 'a distinct feeling of moral or cultural superiority to the rest of society or to particular features of it – for example, industrialism – was a conspicuous element'.[17]

Alderley Edge had its own moral celebrity in James Wood. Its principal, as Gissing was affectionately to recall, would often read to the school before bedtime 'something from Dr Arnold'.[18] And yet the promotion of this distinct feeling of moral superiority and resistance to the rest of society in Gissing's day diverges in a fundamental way from the ends of a liberal education in integrating the personality *with* society in the earlier Georgian period. Moreover the new ideal of 'Culture' invested in the received classical tradition against the fragmentation of society and its mechanical forms of knowledge[19] clearly conflicts with the competitive ends to which, for the aspiring lower-class secondary pupil at least, the traditional classical education was now put.

This conflict of values is evident in the very conditions under which Gissing was to continue his classical studies at Owen's College in Manchester in the early 1870s. Owen's College had grown out of the earlier efforts of the Manchester Literary and Philosophical Society to establish an institution of higher education at Manchester that would be free of religious tests and effectively serve the technical and vocational needs of a predomi- nantly industrial community.[20] The college was planned from the beginning as a primarily scientific institution. Yet Gissing's specialisation in the humanities there – he won exhibitions in Latin and English in the matriculation of the University of London in 1875 – was not in any way eccentric. Significantly, the opening address at the inauguration of the college in 1851 was given by J. G. Greenwood, the Professor of Classics and later long-serving Principal of the college. Professor Greenwood's talk 'On the Languages and Literature of Greece and Rome' reiterates the traditional defence of the classics as useful for the general training of the mind, and significantly as a means of solacing the mind against a contaminating absorption in commercial and industrial pursuits. Since the classics are not likely to be of practical use to a man in later life, Greenwood argues, the more desirable it is that he should cultivate them, so that 'amidst his own engrossing cares he may be allured to converse with the great minds of other times and countries'.[21] It is the classic humanist argument which was to be given new force by Matthew Arnold in the following decade.

The centrality of the classics in Gissing's own intellectual formation, and indeed in the curriculum of a primarily scientific and technical institution, is to be explained by that gradual fusion of conservative and liberal interests in English political

and cultural life. It was a fusion in which, in educational
terms at least, the broad humanism of the eighteenth-century
reformers lost out to an 'institutionalised traditionalism', encouraging specialisation, and promoting through 'culture' the aims
of social consolidation and subordination. State intervention in
the higher-educational sector arose largely in response to the
demands of radicals and Nonconformists in the restructured
society,[22] but the measures adopted were not those advanced
by J. S. Mill and the radical polemicists of the *Westminster Review*
who, earlier in the century, had attacked classicism, clericism
and aristocracy. Rather, reorganisation produced a merging
of the sons of aristocracy and industry in a conjunction of
'aristocratic' and 'bourgeois' interests already foreshadowed in
Thomas Arnold's ideal of 'Christian Gentlemen' while he was
head at Rugby. It was a reorganisation that was to become the
social mainstay of the new Victorian 'Upper-Middle Classes'.[23]

The preservation of the classics as the source of 'universal
knowledge', of what Matthew Arnold came to define as 'the
best that has been known and thought',[24] was an important
aspect of this whole process of cultural consolidation through
a general system of schooling. Arnold's progressive ideal of
awakening in all men the authority of the 'best self' clearly
aimed at establishing the authority of intellectual conscience
and autonomy in the new secular 'bourgeois' state; yet in its
proclaimed sovereignty and self-exemption from the processes
of instrumental rationality, Arnold's idea of 'culture' became,
as Raymond Williams has pointed out, *not* the material process his ideology reached for, but 'more and more . . . an
abstraction'.[25]

The weakness of Arnold's 'critical-Utopian' outlook is nowhere
more evident than in his essentially static, hierarchical view of
'class'. His acceptance of the superiority of the classics, for
instance, while advocating the teaching of English in some
middle- and working-class schools, rested, like the reorganisation
of secondary education itself in the mid-Victorian period, on a
tacit acceptance of traditional social divisions. Arnold failed,
Margaret Mathieson has argued,

> to realise that to some extent, by his support for the reten-
> tion of the traditional classical curriculum for the public
> schools, Latin for older secondary pupils, and English for

the lower-middle-class and elementary school pupils, he was responsible for the perpetuation of class differences.[26]

One might want to alter this to suggest that such support actually institutionalised class differences. The history of nineteenth-century educational reform is evidence of just such a process. The period of active state intervention and reorganisation of all levels of education between 1850 and 1870 was one which saw not only the establishment of different kinds of schooling for different social groups, but the creation of an 'entirely segregated system of education for the governing classes'.[27] This was effectively realised by the reform of the public and endowed schools respectively following the Clarendon (1861) and the Taunton (1864) Commissions.

The conflicting values that were to direct this whole process of reorganisation are reflected with particular intensity in George Gissing's life. It is not that Gissing was idiosyncratic in this respect, the product, as Wells suggests, of 'the insanity of our educational organization' which 'had planted down in that Yorkshire town, a grammar school dominated by the idea of classical scholarship'.[28] The recommendations of the Clarendon Commission had ensured that the classics remained the centre of a liberal education, with science as an important ancillary. It was a recommendation adopted not only by the newly reformed public schools, but by that stratum of aspiring grammar and proprietary schools in which Gissing was to be educated. The claim for the existence of a 'ladder of learning' enabling boys of promise to climb from a humble home to the universities undoubtedly encouraged this process of slavish imitation. Yet such a claim also promoted competition based on the idea of 'testable knowledge' and on 'the development of objective criteria for judging success',[29] principles clearly at odds with the avowed ends of a classical education. For the classics were seen by Arnold and others not only as a means of integrating the personality with society through the refinements of culture, but also of providing solace and moral resistance to the fragmentation and specialisation of a largely competitive civilisation. Moreover the prerequisite of such a ladder is a logical gradation based on standards of education, and not on one's position in society. Yet it was the latter which effectively directed the recommendations of the Taunton Commission. The ladder of learning advocated

by T. H. Green and the Commissioners[30] represents an early
expression of that fallacious argument which would transfer
responsibility for failure from social and economic organisation
to the individual, while at the same time accepting the reality of
existing social inequality. It must be added, as evidence of Green's
own intellectual honesty, that he himself was later to recognise
the fallacy of the Commissioners' ideal, and to lament that
'mischievous' segregation in England 'based on social pretensions'
which 'embarrasses all the schemes of school reformers'.[31]

The tensions of Gissing's exile are rooted in these cultural
contradictions. Culture may have been presented to the aspiring
lower middle-class intellectual such as Gissing as the distinct
organ of the 'best self' – the basis of a corporate intellectual
resistance to the mechanical civilisation – but for such an
aspirant it was also the means of personal validation in that
very society. The expectations of social and spiritual centrality,
of corporate consciousness and occupational rewards were
seriously thwarted, however, by the realities of inherited social
stratification and inequality. To create the kind of 'missionary
of culture' envisaged by Arnold, the new intellectual had to be
raised out of his own class; but he was elevated in this way
to be a social functionary or intermediary, not a social aspirant.

Gissing's own response to the frustrations of entrenched stratification and to the resulting sense of injured dignity was not an
uncommon one. His youthful flirtation with the Positivists and
with contemporary middle-class hopes of cultural transformation
was quickly to give way to a defensive dream of passivity and
inner withdrawal from a hostile and refusing world. 'Keep apart,
keep apart, and preserve one's soul alive', he was to write on
hearing of William Morris's arrest during a political meeting in
the East End, 'that is the teaching of the day. It is ill to
have been born in these times, but one must make a world
within a world.'[32] It is an attitude which Thomas Carlyle had
foreseen would be the trap for those 'speculative' elements of the
intellectual 'aristocracy' or 'unclassed' who would 'fly off into
"Literature", into what they call Art, Poetry, and the like'.[33] For
Gissing it answered to the need for a continuing commitment to
alternative principles. It also served to protect him inwardly from
what Jacob Korg identifies as the 'unexpected hazards and strange
inner conflict of social climbing'.[34] Gissing's refusal of the polite
society to which he had entrance at the homes of the Gaussens

and Harrisons in the early 1880s points away from the kind of explanation that came most easily to Gissing himself in charting his difficulties. It was not simply a question of the cultured mind in unfavourable circumstances, of being among that 'class of young men distinctive of our time – well-educated, fairly bred, but without money'.[35] Nor was it merely a matter of Gissing's uneasiness about his inferior social origins. Rather, Gissing's refusal indicates the hidden injuries that afflict the individual in a 'traditional', stratified society in which one is seen to be answerable nevertheless for one's own condition. It is in effect an authentic response to the trauma of inauthenticity in a liberal age dominated by a new secular morality. The propensity for suffering and 'quite peculiar inability' to be unreservedly happy which Gabrielle Fleury came to know as 'a constitutional feature of his quite in his blood'[36] was at once a symptom of his social injury and the defensive stratagem of one who had already been denied. This protective alienation was also necessary for another reason. For the individual's claim to social and spiritual centrality was only to be won – and this the educational reformers themselves clearly intended[37] – at the cost of his isolation from his own class and community. The fierce and uncompromising attachment to inner selfhood shown by Gissing and his 'unclassed' heroes would seem at times to carry the suggestion of sacrifice and guilty atonement for the betrayal of fraternity, while at the same time it is their very attachment to culture that is being atoned for.

It is a paradox which indicates the peculiar impotence of Gissing's inner emigration. The withdrawn yet resistant Arnoldian self – the basis in effect of Gissing's attempt to resolve ideologically the severe cultural contradictions to which his education and upbringing exposed him – remains harnessed in its innermost repressions to the very circumstances of struggle, envy and desire for possession from which it claims to be free. Culture for Gissing may have signified an inward condition of knowledge, transcending the inadequacies of existing class interests and ideologies, but it was also a socially constitutive feature of his own struggle for existence, materially bound up with the realities of class difference and inherited privilege, as well as with his own social and intellectual ambition.

It is this firmly materialistic edge to Gissing's attachment which critics have tended either to overlook, or else to condemn as a sign of an élitist and unhappy temperament. H. G. Wells, for instance, was unable to see in Gissing's classical education anything more than a regrettable obscurantism that had rendered him incapable of looking life 'squarely in the eye'.[38] This may seem a curious charge to level against a revolutionary writer whose work had played a significant role in freeing the novel from the inhibiting pressures of Victorian public taste. Wells' reference is in fact to Gissing's lack of palate for the 'shrewd humour . . . kindly stoicisms . . . and fantastic and often grotesque generosities which this dear London life of ours exudes'.[39] Yet Gissing's unsympathetic view of modern life is not simply the result of a somewhat pedantic classical education. It rested equally on the knowledge that energetic individualism could not in the end provide a genuine basis of social or intellectual autonomy in a residually aristocratic society. The cramping gentility of Gissing's upbringing was not, in this context, simply that demanded by the repressive conventions and moral standards of Victorian life; it was directed by the imperatives of an acute and crushing class-consciousness in an individualistic, yet still archaic social order. It is a consciousness which indicates not some temperamental egoism or pitiable abnormality, but the disturbing reality of English social and intellectual life.

Although the conditions of Gissing's exile undoubtedly reduced his prospects of personal happiness, they provided an effective standpoint for an important aesthetic interrogation of the society in which he lived. Gissing's intellectual non-conformity may have presented itself as that of the privileged Arnoldian self, of 'the unclassed'; but the still-active association of culture with social refinement and personal ambition in Gissing's work ideologically prevents its liberation from the 'declassing' structures of the classic realist novel, from the need for personal integration with a decisive social world. There is no formal accommodation of the kind of disintegration of society within the self that is found, say, in the work of Henry James and the modernists. Yet given his social marginality in an increasingly organised and oppressive industrial order, Gissing is constrained to subvert the finality of the classic realist conventions in seeking to represent the conditions of his class and his times.

The result of this is in one respect extremely disabling. Readers have often commented on the defeatist nature of Gissing's critique of late-Victorian society. They refer specifically to his static and finally fatalistic vision of human misery and oppression, as well as to the impotence of his absolute distinction between culture and progress. Yet Gissing's subversion of the Romantic structure of the earlier Victorian novel, with its essentially moral solution to the problem of personal and social settlement, is in another respect uniquely effective. For it results in an image of permanent struggle that does not attempt to harlequinise or to colour romantically the harsh realities of lower-class life. In the grouping of characters about some determining influence or force, Gissing's best novels belong, as Wells suggested, to the more 'impersonal type of structure' found in the works of the Continental masters.[40]

More significantly, in turning in upon the basis of its own ironic ethical centre, Gissing's work would seem to make visible a structural deficiency at the heart of English social and intellectual life – the lack of a genuine intellectual independence or corporate identity in the new secular nation state. The possibility of some form of authentic resistance or Bohemian autonomy among the 'new men' who are working for the future is finally discounted by Gissing in a society whose institutions and structures continue to rest on, and to sustain, a residually aristocratic and largely uncontested traditionalism. In his studies of middle-class exile, Gissing unflinchingly exposes the complicity and final fragility of his own cherished ideal of pure and unassailable selfhood. The creation in these works of vivid intellectual types fretfully immersed in the struggles of modern urban life constitutes Gissing's major contribution to the English novel. It is one which closely links his works in a unique way to the traditions of the great European realists. Gissing's radical critique of the new 'bourgeois' social order is rooted, as in European realism, in an intellectual and cultural Utopianism that is firmly social and materialistic in its innermost perspectives.

Given the specifically social pressures of his 'aristocratic credo', Gissing is constrained to refuse the kind of idealist connection between 'human' values and existing society found in the English novel of the classic realist period. At the same time he avoids the tendency of the indigenous English novel of the late-Victorian period and after to rest on a merely external, self-satisfied critique of bourgeois conventionality. The suggestion, however, is not that Gissing's work belongs outside the English tradition. Such a claim ignores the peculiarly English nature of Gissing's intellectual formation, and its unusual formal effects. The social and material dimension that attaches to the idea of culture in Gissing's work not only results in an eschewal of the ironic strategies of resolution found in the traditional English novel; it also undermines the moral basis of Gissing's own privileged ironic focus and claim to authority – the basis of that function which Frederic Jameson has characterised as realism's 'subjective corrosive mission'.[41] The frustration and impasse of Gissing's exile are in this sense translated into the structures of the novel itself to produce a disturbing, alienating art.

Writing specifically about Gissing's social novels, Raymond Williams has suggested that,

> Anyone now in Gissing's position, or in one resembling it, can gain from a critical reading of these social novels, in their exposure of a number of prejudices and false positions, towards which this situation by its own pressures urges them.[42]

His perception is of the possibility of an engagement altogether different from the kind assumed by Frank Swinnerton in contemptuously dismissing Gissing's admirers as 'ill-educated egoists'.[43] It is one which demands the replacement of identification with interrogation, illusion with distance.

Such a position is in fact prefigured in the writings of earlier critics of Gissing's work. Virginia Woolf, for instance, may dismiss this 'imperfect novelist' as the 'favourite . . . of a great many middle-aged, sceptical, rather depressed men and women', but she is constrained to observe and indeed to applaud Gissing's capacity to leave 'the reader whose pleasure it is to identify with the hero or heroine . . . completely baffled'.[44] In an equally percipient critique of Gissing's work, Henry James pleads in the end for the kind of aesthetic unity and cohesion which yields the satisfaction of 'knowledge'.[45] It is the kind of satisfaction which, in James's view, Gissing persistently promises but 'almost as persistently disappoints'.[46] Yet James's bafflement in the face of Gissing's inattention to matters of compositional office and authorial control – a feeling which was to turn to impatience in his later arraignment of Gissing's younger contemporaries[47] – is tempered by an uneasy sense that it is 'just this fact of a question about him' which is 'part of the wonder – I use the word in the sense of enjoyment – that he excites'.[48] It is a recognition which urges, for instance, the whole question of Gissing's problematic relationship with his 'cultured' heroes; indeed, it is this whole problem which James's elaborate technical prescriptions on structural composition would seem finally to repress. It is not, in other words, a question of identifying with Gissing's cultured resistance to an inauthentic world; nor of extolling his vision of struggle and necessity against his own illusory ideals. The antithetical demands of James and Wells have in this context merely been repeated in the oppositional interpretations of later 'humanist' and 'materialist' critics. Rather it is a question of an engagement with the moral irresolution out of which Gissing's novels emerge and in which they come finally to rest. It is this sense of unresolved contradiction, of openness, which this reading of the novels will seek to incorporate. It will be an attempt to respond to the possibilities of a different 'sense of enjoyment' inchoately recognised by James. If such a reading is not confined to Gissing, with Gissing nevertheless we really have no choice. For to impose a moral interpretation on Gissing's work is in the end to blind ourselves to the whole problem of contemplative freedom and intellectual privilege which his novels would force us to question, and which constitutes the whole force of what is being said.

1
Hogarthian Beginnings

> *. . . never a tear comes at Hogarth's call. It is his sentence of everlasting expulsion from the highest heaven of art.*
>
> Mrs Oliphant

The choice by historians and literary critics alike of 1880 as the point at which to date the effective end of that spirit and temper which we generally associate with the adjective 'Victorian' would seem to have a special significance in Gissing's case. In that year, Gissing published his first novel, *Workers in the Dawn*, an impassioned, if structurally diffuse attack on Victorian ideals of progress and social reform. The renewed class antagonisms of the 1870s and the re-entry of the working classes into the political arena; the check to lower-class aspirations that resulted from the increasing fragmentation and specialisation of social and intellectual life: these forces are reflected in the frustrations of the *déclassé* hero Arthur Golding, and in the failure of the middle-class heroine's philanthropic ideal of reform through education.

The subversion of the structures of the traditional Victorian novel and its characteristic progress towards personal and social connection does not of course begin with Gissing. Adrian Poole, in a discerning account of the literary 'context' of Gissing's work, has traced the structural effects of a deepening scepticism in the novels of Gissing's predecessors in the mid-Victorian period.[1] He identifies a growing sense of 'intransigence' in the opposition between the two spheres of inner desire and outer reality, and in an attendant withdrawal in the direction of a more abstract and metaphysical rendering of society and its relation to individual

14

lives.[2] Yet it remains true that in Gissing's work this schism has become one of unprecedented severance that may challenge the essential confidence of the traditional Victorian novel, but has tended to link his deep social pessimism with the formal decline of the indigenous English novel of the transitional and later contemporary era generally. It is a decline that is located in the formal commitment of English writers to narrow naturalistic or impressionistic techniques which fail to grasp and bring to light the inherent possibilities and connections in character and situation.[3] The aim of the present reading will be to claim that far from having a limiting or constricting effect, Gissing's sceptical view of social reform – his refusal of these 'reformist-interventionist' images of man's common brotherhood found in the earlier Victorian novel – produces in his first novel the beginnings of a uniquely unidealised picture of the urban poor. More importantly the exposed inadequacies of liberal humanist values in meeting individualist and corporate demands in the new secular social order will be shown to open up, in the hero's journey of discovery, an image of deadlock and intellectual exile. The hero's defeat comes to symbolise not only the failure of middle-class hopes of reform, but the insufficiency of inner withdrawal. It is a disclosure which shall be seen in the end to undermine the authority of the novel's own critical perspective in a way that disturbs the satisfactions of identification and contemplative moral privilege common to the processing operations of narrative memesis within which Gissing writes. Indeed, it is the final absence of an idealising or sentimental perspective which links Gissing's realism with the art of Hogarth, whose robustness and unflinching delineation of life Gissing strove to bring to the English novel.

The extent of Gissing's debt to Hogarth is indicated by his friend Eduard Bertz in one of the first comprehensive studies of Gissing's novels.[4] In *Workers in the Dawn*, the 'Hogarthian' influence is evident in certain thematic features – the progress of the failed artist and the unregenerate prostitute, for instance; and in the contemporary cynicism of Maud Gresham's 'marriage à-la-mode' with its unholy alliance of commerce and respectability hostile to human values. Yet the importance of the Hogarthian influence does not lie in the sum of Hogarthian themes and images in the work. It is to be located in Gissing's conscious moral and artistic purpose. Gissing, of course, is not unique in this respect. 'Hogarth's painting,' as Mario Praz has shown, although

> closely connected with the literature, particularly the satirical literature, of the age . . . does also anticipate the nineteenth-century novel, especially that of Dickens, with his satirical portraits and his impressions of the London slums.[5]

Indeed one literary historian has traced a fruitful interaction and creative exchange between the direct heirs to Hogarth's art of graphic satire, such as George Cruikshank and H. K. Browne, and the monthly part novelists.[6] Both Victorian novelists and their illustrators adapted from Hogarth that combination of popular entertainment and morality which was to attain such a hold on an increasingly literate public. In his 'Preface' to *Oliver Twist*, Dickens openly acknowledged Hogarth 'the moralist, and censor of his age' as one of his examples and precedents, an admission to those critics who, from the first, had linked his name with Hogarth's.[7]

Yet as Gissing was later to recognise, it is precisely the uncompromising spirit of Hogarth's art that is modified by the sentimentality and popular comic spirit of the Dickensian vision:

> Try to imagine a volume of fiction produced by the artist of *Gin Lane*, of *The Harlot's Progress*, and put it beside the books which, from Pickwick onwards, have been the delight of English homes. Puritans both of them, Hogarth shows his religion on the sterner side; Dickens, in a gentle avoidance of whatsoever may give offence to the pure of heart, the very essence of his artistic conscience being that compromise which the other scorned. In truth, as artists they saw differently. Dickens was no self deceiver; at any moment his steps would guide him to parts of London where he could behold, and had often beheld, scenes as terrible as any that the artist struck into black and white; he looked steadily at such things, and, at the proper time, could speak of them. But when he took up the pen of the story-teller, his genius constrained him to such use, such interpretation, of bitter fact as made him beloved, not dreaded, by readers asking, before all else, to be soothingly entertained.[8]

Gissing's own desire to produce a combative, unsentimental fiction thus comes to measure not only his identification with

Hogarth, but his distance from Dickens. John Goode has referred in this context to the picture that announced Dickens's death, 'The Empty Chair': it was not that Gissing failed to fill it, but that he was determined not to.[9] 'One cannot, of course compare my method and aims with those of Dickens', Gissing was to write after the publication of *Workers in the Dawn*. 'I mean to bring home to people the ghastly condition (material, mental, moral) of our poor classes, to show the hideous injustice of our whole system of society, and to give light upon a plan of altering it.'[10]

Workers in the Dawn is clearly an attempt to satisfy the need for a critical art expressing protest and indignation to which Mr Tollady, the hero's surrogate father and Dantean guide through the urban inferno, gives voice:

> 'Be a successor of Hogarth, and give us the true image of *our* social dress, as he did of those of his own day. Paint them as you see them, and get your picture hung in the Academy. It would be a moral lesson to all who looked upon it, surpassing in value every sermon that fanaticism has ever concocted!' (I.I.xi, 164)

Arthur's inability to respond to his teacher's directive is symptomatic of the historical gulf that separates them. He is a child of an industrial age rooted in the disabling polarisation of fact and value. His interpretation of the artistic strategy urged by Mr Tollady manifests the very dualism his teacher would have him overcome. He feels his artistic impulses checked by Mr Tollady's notion of a committed art, and ends by rejecting Hogarth's 'hideousness' for a devotion to beauty which his inner voice dictates. It is this opposition of art and social commitment which lies behind his feelings of a 'double life':

> As he grew older he felt within himself the stirrings of a double life, the one, due to his natural gifts, comprehending all the instincts, the hopes, the ambitions of the artist; the other, originating in the outward circumstances of his childhood . . . which urged him on to the labours of the philanthropist, showing him in the terribly distinct reflex of his own imagination the ever-multiplying miseries of the poor amongst whom he lived. (I.I.xi, 158)

Art and creativity are here mystified as 'natural' impulses independent of outward circumstances. Aesthetics, for Arthur, has become synonymous with aestheticism.

It would be wrong to identify the hero's views on art with those of his creator. Arthur's painting may express genuine feeling as opposed to the society artist Gilbert Gresham's fashionable productions; but opposed to both is Gissing himself and the novel he writes. It is not so much that *Workers in the Dawn* seems to 'postulate "art" as something entirely unconscious of his own novel's existence'.[11] Rather the novel would seem to offer itself – to use the phraseology of the Hungarian critic Georg Lukács's Hegelian study of the novel[12] – as the point of 'irony' or 'self-correction' of the debased world in which the hero is marooned.

Although we are given no extended account of Arthur's art, we nevertheless learn of the two paintings inspired by Helen's reading of Tennyson's 'The Palace of Art' that 'there lurked a spell' which was 'at once seized captive sympathetic souls and bound them to a daydream of glimmering fancies'(II.III.ix). It is significant that Arthur's final rejection of social commitment should take place at this point. The implication is that he has surrendered to the temptations of withdrawal which, as Helen recognises, it is the poem's moral to deprecate. The ironic novelist, in other words, dissociates himself from the hero's aestheticism. His own novel does not aim to produce 'a daydream of glimmering fancies'. It is intended as a 'Hogarthian' work.

The description of Whitecross Street on Christmas Eve, for example, presents an image of the unbridgeable gulf between rich and poor which contrasts sharply with the traditional Dickensian notion of Christmas (I.I.v). The celebration of Christmas at the Pettidunds, later in the novel, is an occasion for drunkenness and squalid excess which provides a Hogarthian back-drop to the discovery of Carrie's dead child and the beginning of Arthur's sordid enslavement to the psychology of sympathy and sacrifice (I.II.xii). There is no suspension of injustice and misery in the ritual giving of gifts. Arthur's gift does not establish a mutual harmony between giver and receiver, but binds both in a twisted web of sexual and social coercions and humiliations. Here as elsewhere the novel exposes the social significance of the gift. John Pether, the radical most sensitive to the hidden injuries of class, bitterly explains it to the novel's philanthropic heroine:

'Do you know that every penny you give in charity, as you call it, is poison to the poor, killing their independence and that sense of liberty which is the only possession they can

hope to boast of? Do you know that you accustom them to
think of you rich as the lawful holders of all the fruits of the
earth, from whom they must be glad to receive what scanty
crumbs it pleases you to throw to them, when they ought
rather to rise as one man and demand as an eternal right what
you pride yourself in giving them as a boon?'   (I.II.vii, 369–70)

Pether clearly recognises the status-maintaining function of charity and its demoralising effects.

It is this aspect of the novel – its exposure of the failure
of charity and sympathy as remedies for social misery – that
Adrian Poole has chosen to emphasise.[13] The scenes describing
Bill Blatherwick's professional mendicity are intended, he argues,
as a criticism of philanthropic attitudes assumed as 'natural' in
the works of Mrs Gaskell and George Eliot, and indeed among
Gissing's own contemporaries. Criticism of philanthropy does in
fact run much further back and had already begun to harden in
the mid-Victorian period.[14] Indeed it is the demoralising effects
of indiscriminate alms-giving and the segregation of the classes
in London which the novel's heroine, Helen Norman, and
her clergyman helper, Mr Heatherley, strive unsuccessfully
to overcome. Their programme of reform displays that curious mixture of scientific purposefulness and encouragement to
self-reliance whose failure was already evident by the close of
the 1870s when the novel was written.[15] The novel, in other
words, does not simply offer a correction or reversal of an
antecedent attitude – in this instance, a critique of charity
that recognises its demoralising effects. Directing the novel is
an overriding pessimism and sense of urban degeneration that
lies beyond explicit correctives to middle-class philanthropy.

This mood is given a variety of expressions in the novel.
Challenging the view that social misery is the result of the
'actual cruelty and oppression of the higher ranks of society',
the artist Gilbert Gresham transfers responsibility to the poor by
blaming their condition on their own 'persistent self brutaliza-
tions'(I.II.i). A more deterministic vision of urban degeneration
is voiced by the peripatetic Tollady:

'Look at that old woman, scarcely three feet high. What a monster of deformity. What generations of toil-worn, vice-blasted,

hunger-nipped wretches has it taken to produce a scion such
as that. . . . Is it not a disgrace to humanity that generations of
servitude, as real and degrading as that of the negroes, should
be suffered to produce in the centre of our proudest cities
a breed of men and women such as these we have been
observing, absolute Calibans, for the most part, in respect
of a pure type of human strength and beauty?'   (I.I.xi, 163–4)

It is this pervasive sense of deterioration which partly motivates
the novel's own radical polemic against the optimistic solutions
of the intelligentsia of the 1860s and 1870s to the problem
of the 'two nations'. And yet the tendency of this vision to
assume that the achieved state of civilization has effectively
passed would seem in a paradoxical way to undermine the
ethical basis of the novel's own Hogarthian purpose.

This conflict is also evident on another level. Although Gissing
himself rightly minimised the influence of Continental revolutionary propaganda in England,[16] his warnings of the 'dangerous
fanaticism' of the 'Party' undoubtedly reflected the uneasy attitude of the middle classes in general in the depressed 1870s
to the demands of the British labour movement for a politics independent of the Liberal Party and existing institutions.[17]
Gissing's own response to the threat of anarchy was an insistence
on the need to educate the masses.[18] But although Gissing
would seem consciously to identify with the educational zeal of
those 'earnest young people striving for improvement in . . . the
dawn of a new phase of civilization',[19] his novel clear-sightedly
confronts the insufficiency of education and culture as solutions
to the personal and social crisis facing its hero and heroine
as young people educated in the 1860s. Arthur Golding and
Helen Norman together with Maud Gresham and Augustus
Wiffle form a youthful quaternity within which the educational
theories of the older generation are tested and found wanting.

For Orlando Wiffle, who serves as curate to Helen's father, the
challenge of industry and science to the authority of the Christian
State appears unproblematic. The poor are seen as mere *tabulae
rasae* to be instructed in the inviolable and undifferentiated laws
of Church and State (I.I.ii). His absolutism is reflected in a scho-
lastic, mechanical mode of instruction. Its very inappropriateness
to a pluralistic age produce in his son Augustus mere canting and
hypocrisy. It is an indication of the novel's satirical zest that this

future ecclesiastic should become involved with Maud Gresham, Gilbert Gresham's cynical, nihilistic daughter, whose education at a London ladies' school has been in 'externals' rather than 'culture'. Augustus is the first in a long line of charlatans who inhabit Gissing's fictional world: Vincent Lacour, Jasper Milvain, Bruno Chilvers. The spirit of Pecksniff is here given a psychological bearing. For Gissing's charlatans the inner and the outer worlds are always separate. Indeed, it is their very capacity to separate them which guarantees their survival in an individualistic age still bound to moral formulae. Augustus Wiffle's hypocrisy is presented as the unheroic, that is to say the practical but morally inadequate solution to the hero's crippling dualism. In parallel fashion, Maud Gresham's cultivation of outward forms is shown to be the antithesis of the moral earnestness of Helen's inner culture.

Helen's father is drawn in his crisis of conscience neither to the orthodoxy of his curate, nor to the relativistic 'decency of outward forms' advocated by Gilbert Gresham. Mr Norman's attachment is to a moral aestheticism overlaid with Hellenism and Epicurean detachment. His instruction of Helen is marked by an Arnoldian emphasis on poetry and 'the development of the emotional part of the child's nature':

> To know the poets, those who are unquestionably great in all ages, to read them with facility in the tongue they wrote in, this was the great end of his educational scheme. For inasmuch as poetry represents the highest phase of emotional activity, in that degree does it deserve to take a foremost place among the influences which may be relied upon for the moulding of the female character into the noblest form of which earth has knowledge.   (I.I.ix, 127–8)

The evident lack of irony at this point would seem to indicate the direction of the novelist's own sympathies. And yet Helen's encounter with the ungrateful workman makes clear the limitations of an attachment which remains 'ignorant of the pains and passions which convert earth's sanctuaries into dreary realms of chaos and black night'.

In terms of the novel's educational debate, the opposition between Wiffle and Norman serves to distinguish between the former's 'positivism' and hierarchy, as the hypostasis of a religious absolutism, and the latter's élitist aestheticism, which is its metaphysical substitute. Wiffle and Norman in other words can be seen to represent that false antithesis within the positivistic circle – positivism–aestheticism – which excludes a view of knowledge and human existence embracing both fact *and* value. It is from this circle that the novel's heroine seeks to escape through an unlikely fusion of Comte and Schopenhauer, and from which, as we shall see, both hero and heroine are ultimately unredeemed.

Helen's record of her intellectual development while abroad recapitulates the philosophical origins of the 'religion of humanity' which emerged in the 1860s among the English middle-class intelligentsia. Her mission to the East End of London reflects that change from *laissez-faire* to corporate notions of society characteristic of this decade onwards, a return to Ruskin by way of T. H. Green's radical socialism which was to inspire Arnold Toynbee and the University Extension of the 1870s, and reached its peak in the Settlement Movement of the following decade.[20]

Helen's intellectual emancipation begins with her reading of Strauss. Her subsequent attempt to reconcile science and Christianity has its parallel in contemporary latitudinarianism. both in its reaffirmation of scientific progress and in its attempted supersession of her moral aesthetic inheritance. Her laying aside of imagination points in fact to a real opposition from Broad Church liberals such as T. H. Green to Arnold's 'religion of culture';[21] although for both the real enemy was utilitarianism. Helen's ultimate agnosticism is sealed by her reading of Darwin. Her search for a rational faith is thus circumscribed by the crippling rationalisms of 'higher criticism' and natural science. The cobbling together of Comte and Schopenhauer which finally supports her 'religion of humanity' reaffirms two aspects of her latitudinarian endeavour – progress and ethical demand. Her latitudinarian opposition to individualism finds its secular analogue in Schopenhauer's vision of a society of conquered egotisms whose ethical basis is located in man's mutual pity before the unpitying void.[22] Moreover the correlation of ethics and aesthetics in Schopenhauer's view of artistic contemplation accommodates Helen's legacy of Arnoldian aesthetics. Her final eclectic fusion of Schopenhauer's ethics and Comte's science of human life is an attempt to heal that division opening up between fact and value in the modern mind.

This reconciling of Comte and Schopenhauer also represents an attempt to develop a radical theoretical alternative to a combination of empirical methodology and traditional ideology which dominated English intellectual life. Helen's fusion of positivism and aestheticism fails to produce a genuine radical theory; its consequence is a mere pragmatism combining fact and value, science and art in a 'philosophy of life' that glosses the initial dualism it seeks to overcome. The implicitly abstract epistemologies of both 'objectivist' positivism and 'phenomenological' aestheticism, in failing to recognise the social foundation of knowledge and value, result in practice in a hierarchy and élitism in harmony with the existing structures of authority and control. Helen's religion of humanity, like T. H. Green's idealism and Matthew Arnold's ethical criticism, is thus in the end merely another conservative reformist solution to the threat of democracy.

Workers in the Dawn exposes the inadequacy of its heroine's reformist programme and attempt to achieve an intellectual autonomy. Yet that Helen's position is similar to Gissing's own is evident in the novel's treatment of two historical events: the resurgence of working-class radicalism in England at the time of the Paris Commune; and the passing of the Education Act of 1870 which formulated a general acceptance of the necessity of elementary education for the poor. The first is represented in the novel as a potential threat to social order; the second is offered as a possible solution to injustice and the legitimacy of working-class demands. Arthur's speech to the working-man's club on hearing of the establishment of the new French Republic is an appeal not for revolutionary consciousness, but for the provision of state education for the poor (II.II.xi). His social commitment, like Helen's secular mission to the East End, is presented in terms of that spirit of sympathy and conscience which provided a contemporary rationale for social reform and missionary movements throughout the 1870s. Indeed, it is just such humanitarian feeling that would seem to direct the novelist's own aim of awakening social conscience and encouraging reform. Yet the predominant attitude to working-class life in *Workers in the Dawn* is one not of sympathy, but of fear. The novel attempts to put this fear to rest in the lurid death of the extremist, John Pether, who dies in delirium after the defeat of the Commune (II.III.iii). The fear of anarchy resurfaces, however, in the spectacle of Carrie, the 'reviving animal' unresponsive to education, plotting with her low-life companions for Arthur to 'kick the bucket' (II.III.xiv).

It is this unconquered fear which marks the departure of *Workers in the Dawn* from the ideology of the earlier 'social problem' novel. In the 'social problem' or 'industrial' novels of the 1840s and 1850s, middle-class fear of the demos is ultimately put to rest in the spectacle of efficacious sympathy – in, say, the return to reason and sovereignty in *Sybil*, or in the recantations of *Alton Locke*. In *Workers in the Dawn* it is the inadequacy of sympathy and middle-class concern itself which comes under scrutiny. The novel's pervasive image of a brutalised poor, and uneasiness in the face of resurgent socialism, serve to demystify the idealism of corporate hopes.

It is Helen's sense of the 'horrible difference of caste' which daunts and finally marks the failure of her 'sanguine hopes of reform':

> 'They will not trust me. My speech, my dress, perhaps, revolts them. They think that I do not belong to their class, and, though they take my money, it is with a suspicion of my motives. I have made my dress as plain as it possibly can be, to be respectable. If I could, I would even speak in their uncouth tongue. There is always that horrible difference of caste between us.'   (II.II.ix, 26)

Helen puts the failure of her social mission down to the barriers created by the external differences of speech and dress. Arthur's Pygmalion-like effort to render Carrie 'more worthy of his devotion' is seen to fail not simply because of a resistance to externals, but because of a mechanism of hidden injury that reaches deeper than the reformers know.

Arthur's educational enterprise is displayed in the antagonism of class relations. His élitist and hierarchical notion of 'deficit'; his attempt to develop Carrie's sensibilities through poetry: these serve only to alienate and humilate because they absolutise middle-class standards of culture as a means of social control. Carrie, as the recipient of Arthur's contractual love, is driven into a sado-masochistic cycle rooted in class conflict. Indeed it is Carrie's own acceptance of her cultural inadequacy which forces her into war not only with an oppressive society, but with herself. Arthur would seem finally to express Gissing's own pessimistic view of reform:

He had glimpses in time of the great truth that education, and education only, working perhaps through generations towards the same end, gaining here a point and there a point, could be the instrument of the redemption of the well-to-do labouring classes.   (II.II.viii, 6)

The final qualification marks the severe restriction of that hope. Yet it is a concession which the novel endorses in the socio-cultural elevation of Lucy Venning, the daughter of a well-to-do working man. In the midst of failure, the novel rehearses an image of success. Yet Lucy's aspirations are realised only by her separation from 'home' and absorption in middle-class mores as Helen's companion. Helen eradicates her working-class defects of speech and manners in order to facilitate her ultimate triumph in gaining Mr Heatherley's declaration. It is doubly ironic that the novel's single success, in its image of separation and difference, should not only dispel any real hope of educating and moralising the poor, but should preserve the very ideal of culture whose inadequacy as a means of social reform and intellectual autonomy the novel itself has so effectively exposed.

What the reader is forced to confront in the end is Gissing's own adherence to the cultural absolutism which dooms his hero to the crippling dualism of his 'double life'. We have already indicated the novel's rejection of Arthur's 'daydream of glimmering fancies'. It is a refusal of the very notion of the work of art as an autonomous, self-regulating artefact. In *Workers in the Dawn* art and culture are seen to depend on labour power and freedom from 'grinding toil'; they are aligned with the privileges of wealth and class. Helen, who fires his devotion to art, is also for Arthur the image of social distance. This potentially radical configuration is suppressed, however, in the separation of politics and aesthetics encoded in Arthur's alternation between Will Noble, the working-class leader with an anti-aesthetic reverence for facts, and Helen, with her ahistorical vision of art and creative genius:

'We who toil on from day to day doing our little best to lessen the sum of the world's misery are doing good work, it cannot be denied; but what is this compared with the labour of men of genius, labour the result of which stands as milestones on the highway of civilization, each one marking a great and appreciable advance?'   (II.III.vii, 268)

The distinction is between the practical heroes who follow the spirit of the age, and the artistic geniuses who create it. Helen's identification of Arthur with the latter is one that the novel itself ultimately refuses. Rather, he is seen to stray into an aestheticism which falls short of art's potentiality. It is this place which the novel itself tries to fill. But Gissing's Hogarthian challenge to the collusions between the writer and his public which he identified in Dickens's novels is ultimately an impossible attempt to establish a radical social function for art within the fundamental dualism which directs the novel's representations. The novel's Hogarthian programme is denied authority because this could only be located in precisely those liberal humanist values which are shown to be inadequate. The novel fails in effect to tell the reader how to arrive at the means of the reform which its criticisms urge. It is this final lack of conviction which exasperated early reviewers. They recoiled from Gissing's lack of proportion or humour in its largest sense. Like Edith Sichel, they shut his books, 'convinced that, according to Gissing, any effort is failure, idealism a lovable folly, the practical philanthropist an impossibility . . . and culture, above all, an irretrievable mistake'.[23]

Workers in the Dawn manifests in its inner structure a recognition of the beginnings of that breakdown in liberal humanist values characteristic of late-nineteenth-century realism. The problematic hero's search for authentic values not only runs up against the intractabilities of an inauthentic world, but also against the inadequacy of aestheticism and the claims of the inner self. The result is an impasse which the ironic distance exercised by the novelist cannot resolve or supersede. Gissing's Hogarthian challenge to the materialism of industrial society exposes, through its examination of the new intellectual, the ineffectualness of those very liberal humanist values which constitute the ethical basis of its own aesthetic distance. The hero's vocation of resistance against a debased and refractory world ends neither in heroic passivity, nor in the securities of aesthetic cultivation. Rather, it leads to a deadlock within the self from which the novel finally releases him in a Romantic and theatrical suicide.

This sense of inner deadlock, of a subjective self rotting from within, is an emergent feature of late-nineteenth-century realism. Gissing's exiled intellectuals cannot be divorced from that whole process of social and literary change which produced the 'superfluous man' of Russian literature, or the subjectively created world of Flaubert's Madame Bovary. Georg Lukács has argued that the revolutionary traumas of 1848 in Europe, which displaced the bourgeois class from its radical position as the liberators of society as a whole, produced a general ideological crisis among its intelligentsia.[24] Forced into a narrower class allegiance, its artists and writers were inhibited in the authentic representation of reality, of that progressive interaction of individual and social forces which had characterised the revolutionary phase of bourgeois realist art. Without agreeing with Lukács's prescriptive devaluation of bourgeois literature after 1848, one can see that the drift towards subjectivism in art and to the monumental rendering of society in European naturalism has its parallel in the gradual breakdown of those prevalent images of settlement and reconciliation which characterise the English novel until the middle of the century. In the later nineteenth century, the artist and intellectual hero, wrestling between the life of the mind and an intransigent social world, move more and more to the problematic centre of the novel.

It is important to recognise that this perceived isolation is often rooted in the real social conditions of marginalisation experienced by the emergent intellectual in an increasingly stratified and bureaucratic social order. In Europe, and particularly in England, the problem of the emergent intellectual without the autonomy or social position promised by his education originated largely through the whole process of industrialisation and expansion of education. Indeed, Victor Brombert has attempted to explain the preponderance of intellectual types in the French novel as a reflection of this social phenomenon, which produced a growing 'army of failures'.[25] In England the Christian socialist, Scott Holland, one of the inspirers of the Settlement Movement, was to refer in 1891 to the 'social problem of the surplus of educated gentlemen'.[26] Yet the problem of the new intellectual who was to emerge in England with the spread of education was not simply one of surplus. In Russia the intelligentsia had confronted from the first the whole question of feudalism. In France the confrontation between bourgeoisie and aristocracy had been the hallmark of the revolution of 1789. In England by contrast, the ultimate triumph of 'a version of the aristocratic-gentry culture' which resulted from the Glorious Revolution of 1689 was to be reflected in the dependent rather than the assured position of intellectuals in England, and in 'the narrowness of the range of sympathy and curiosity of the British intelligentsia within its own society'.[27] The gradual fusion of aristocratic and bourgeois interests which characterised the emergence of the new industrial society in England resulted, according to Antonio Gramsci, in the failure of the English industrial middle classes to create from their ranks a category of 'organic' intellectuals 'endowed with a character of their own'.[28] The Positivists, for example, scarcely qualify for the title of 'organic' bourgeois intellectuals in Gramsci's specific sense of the term. Even the Fabians, who perhaps came closest to attaining that stature, drew on the heritage of Bentham and Carlyle, rather than on the sociological traditions of Europe, in formulating their programme of gradual reform.[29] The liberal humanist tradition transmitted through the nineteenth-century cultural critics remained the main channel of social and ethical protest in England.

In the early phase of nineteenth-century realism in England, the rupture between the hero's search for authentic values and the degraded society in which his search takes place[30] is generally resolved by an imaginary supersession, provided by the novelist's ironic distance and informed by liberal humanist values. This is true even in the work of so confirmed a Tory as Charlotte Brontë. In *Jane Eyre*, for instance, the pattern of resolution takes the form of an heroic self-suppression, leading, in the marriage of Jane and Rochester, to the moral reformation of a higher social stratum. In the novels of George Eliot this imaginary supersession is forced increasingly from an ideal of the organic world of rural England into the path of conscious symbolism and authorial intervention. It is this ironic privilege which Gissing's *Workers in the Dawn* would seem to be denied in its recognition of the insufficiency of liberal humanism as the basis either of intellectual autonomy or of the defence of order. Yet in the absence of a genuinely 'organic' intellectual tradition, Gissing is unable to transcend the liberal heritage of the traditional realist novel with its ultimate sense of adequate community.

This is particularly evident in Gissing's continuing adherence in *Workers in the Dawn* to the conventional motif of dispossession common to the earlier Victorian novel. The motif of the dispossessed hero, cultured by heredity but blocked by circumstance, embodied that 'underlying assumption of a definite relation

between property and human quality' which, in Raymond
Williams's view, is already questioned in the novels of George
Eliot.[31] In *Oliver Twist* or Disraeli's *Sybil*, for example, it provides
an occasion for a critique of society which nevertheless prepares
for a formal return to order and sovereignty at the close.
In *Workers in the Dawn*, it must be said, the convention
also generates what Karl Mannheim, in a different context,
has classified as the 'double scepticism' that emerges when

> two different horizons impinge on the same person and when
> two opposite creeds of equal vehemence lay claim to him.
> Such a double view of things is often the result of a spatial
> coincidence of consecutive beliefs . . . a situation in which
> an older group continues to advocate an earlier tenet while a
> rising group advances a new one. An individual who has lost
> his security in either group . . . discovers the perplexing fact
> that the same things have different meanings. This puzzlement
> marks the origins of a genuine epistemology, which is more
> than a mere justification of a preconceived idea.[32]

Mannheim's characterisation of the emergence of a radical
intelligentsia is clearly applicable to Gissing's account of Arthur's
'double life'. Yet although the novel's refusal to restore the dispossessed hero constitutes the basis of its revolutionary consciousness, the reason given for that refusal is curiously reactionary:

> The secret of his life lay in the fact that he was an ill-balanced
> nature, lacking that element of a firm and independent will
> which might at any moment exert its preponderance in situa-
> tions of doubt. Hence it resulted that he was one of those men
> whose lives seem to have little result for the world save as
> useful illustrations of the force of circumstance – one of those
> who, had Fortune directed his path amid congenial scenes,
> might have developed a rich individuality.   (II.III.xiv, 378)

We encounter here a key paradox. One the one hand, the novel
exposes the social and ideological nature of the hero's failure to
develop a 'rich individuality'; on the other hand, the voice of
authorial intervention represents his 'double life' as a personal
failure of independent will, and his final exile as a mere consequence of overriding circumstance. The shift, in its contradictory

mixture of secular moralist and environmentalist argument, is from a criticism of society to an affirmation of the salutary effects of wealth and privilege within the existing social order. This is in part a reflex of the motif of dispossession with its assumption of a natural moral order; but it resurfaces in Gissing's later novels which move in their problematic engagement with intellectual exile to the patterns of the *Bildungsroman*, and finally, in the 1890s, to the theme of a 'career'. It would seem to mark the impasse of the novelist and his heroes, doomed to identify the denying authority fatalistically with overriding circumstance, and to revert to the division of inner culture and outward circumstance whose inadequacy the novels themselves so trenchantly expose.

On the face of it this position would seem to be a particularly disabling one. What I have tried to show, however, is how Gissing's very lack of imaginary supersession disturbs the satis-factions of contemplative approaches to narrative mimesis in a way that provides a series of unique insights into the historical and social conflicts that his fictional world would seek to resolve. We have seen, for instance, how *Workers in the Dawn* not only makes fearfully visible the deeper psychological mechanisms of working-class resistance that challenges all hopes of the reformers, but exposes the guilty collusions of cultural aspiration. Although the vision of working-class characters at war not only with society but with themselves would seem ultimately to comfort a conservative position, the image of a divided and dispossessed hero prevents a resolution in organic and conservative ideals of community, or in élitist 'petty-bourgeois' affirmations of moral superiority. The novel itself remains lodged in a 'double scepticism' that exposes an unresolved conflict between radical and conservative impulses at the heart of English intellectual life. From the structural diffusions of this first novel emerges the subject of Gissing's fiction – the new lower middle-class intellectual who must serve an ideal organic community to which he has no entrance; yet who is unable, because of the division of fact and value, to theorise his *malaise*.

2

Residues of Romance

At first, indeed, the illusion dominates the disappointment.

H. G. Wells

In the past, critics have tended to consider Gissing in the 1880s primarily as a writer of 'social problem' novels. The result has been the relative neglect of two significant early novels – *Isabel Clarendon* and *A Life's Morning*. Indeed the dismissal of these works and the identification of the young Gissing's strength with the description of low-life scenes goes back as far as Meridith, who read *Isabel Clarendon* in manuscript.[1] Where criticism has stressed the significance of these novels in the development of Gissing's study of lower middle-class life, it has tended to view them, with *The Unclassed*, merely as flawed, if occasionally interesting anticipations of Gissing's more successful novels of the 1890s.[2] The present contention is not that these works are unqualified successes – they are each marred to different degrees by distorting, melodramatic influences; rather the argument is that they deserve greater consideration than they at present enjoy, for they advance our understanding not only of Gissing's world, but of Victorian fiction and society generally. Close analysis is undertaken in the belief that each of these novels yields its own valuable insights into the problem of lower middle-class exile which pervades Gissing's work. Common to all is an attempt to supersede the failure of the idealist conscience of their 'petty bourgeois' intellectual protagonists through a contrived resolution borrowed from romance – in *The Unclassed* by a reversion to the inheritance plot; in *Isabel Clarendon* and *A Life's Morning* by a return

31

to a version of the *Bildungsroman* in their linking of heroic passivity and moral superiority. The effect in each case is one of severe aesthetic disruption, since the preservation of the ideal in these works involves a regression to the very forms of conventionality which Gissing's realist project has shown to be insufficient. Yet the importance of these works is not to be located in any deliberate straining of the conventional story line such as one finds in Hardy; it is to be ascribed to their reluctant subversion of their own idealist centre. The result is a series of disturbing insights into the hidden injuries and unresolved traumas of lower-class life in England that is unique to these works, and which Gissing's fictional contrivances try mythically to dispel.

I   RITUALS OF ATONEMENT: *THE UNCLASSED*

The Unclassed (1884), Gissing's second published novel, reflects his temporary absorption in Schopenhauerian ideals in the early 1880s, and the consequent weakening of his hopes of reform. The opening chapters are devoted to an almost Zolaesque rendering of the environmental and hereditary formation of the two contrasted personalities who will later symbolise the hero's conflicting aspirations. Ida Starr, with her love of animals and wild nature, is a Rousseauistic *ingénue*, a symbol of natural development unhampered by respectability. By contrast, the respectable and wholly conventional Maud Enderby is raised in an atmosphere of cold religiosity, her attitudes shaped by a residual pre-Enlightenment view of the child as an incomplete adult in need of discipline to curb the imperfections of Original Sin. The hero's dilemma is made explicit later:

> He needed some strong, vehement, original nature, such as Ida Starr's; how would Maud's timid conventionality – doubtless she was absolutely conventional – suit with the heresies of which he was all compact?   (XIV, 111)

Osmond Waymark's dilemma would seem to repeat Arthur Golding's choice in *Workers in the Dawn*; the resemblance, however, turns out to be more apparent than real. In the earlier novel, Helen and Carrie correspond to the ideal and the actual of the hero's aestheticist impasse. In addition Helen represents an ideal of transcendent culture which is seen at the same time to depend on a position of wealth and privilege from which Arthur is excluded. Indeed it is this which disturbs the attempt in the novel to separate culture from circumstance. In *The Unclassed*, by contrast, Maud stands in a more limited way for a social ideal of cultured refinement that resists the spirit of her times; Ida for a spiritual ideal of inner culture transcending circumstance. 'Each answered', we are told, 'to an ideal which he cherished, and the two ideals were so diverse, so mutually exclusive' (XII).

There is in effect a simplification of the crisis represented in the earlier novel. This is also evident in the literary dialogues between Waymark and the novel's shadow-hero, the impractical and weakly sympathetic Julian Casti. Initially the aesthetic debate promises to be rich and searching. The contrast between the two is not that of the autonomous genius creating works 'which stand as milestones on the highway of civilization' and the popular artist serving the market, but the Keatsian one of the 'poet' and the 'dreamer'. There is no explicit reference to Keats's theory in the novel, but Waymark's aesthetic of the impersonal artist in the face of human misery echoes Keats's account of the 'Poet' in the second 'Hyperion' (XXV). This impression is reinforced when Casti identifies himself with the dreamer-poet:

'isn't there a certain resemblance between my case and that of Keats? He too was a drug pounder; he liked it as little as I do; and he died young of consumption. I suppose a dying man may speak the truth about himself. I too might have been a poet, if life had dealt more kindly with me.' (XXXV, 288)

Casti's aestheticism marks a retreat from the conflicts and miseries of industrial society. His 'Romanus sum' in the back of the chemist shop is the cry of the dreamer glorying in Plutarch and the ideal world of classicism. Yet his epic on the capture of Rome by Alaric, which he refers to mysteriously as his 'work', is seen in the novel not as an anachronism but as a spiritual labour heroically opposed to the market.

The implication of the novel's less than ironic view of the poor lodging-house in Walcot Square as a 'temple of the Muses' is that Casti's failure is to be attributed not to the immaturity and incongruity of his form and subject matter, but to the vulgarity of the market, and to the suppression of culture and the poetic spirit by circumstance – specifically by the need to earn money, and by the debilitating contingencies of his unsuitable marriage to the vindictive and vulgar Harriet Smales. Harriet's malicious jealousy refuses both the cultural élitism of her husband's devotion to the classics, and the idealism of his admiration for Ida Starr. Just as Helen's portrait is a source of humiliation to Carrie in *Workers in the Dawn*, so Ida is unwisely offered to Harriet as a humiliating rebuke to her malevolent nature. Although trapped in a self-destructive cycle of injured pride, Harriet, like Carrie, reflects Gissing's fear of that ruthless struggle which challenges the legitimacy of self-sacrifice as a response to social injury. Yet by splitting off the shadow-hero from contact with the world of privilege and class refinement, the novel is able to endorse the opposition of culture and circumstance without the intervening complication of class stratification found in *Workers in the Dawn*. Casti, Ida, Harriet: these reduplicate the conflict of Hero-Ideal-Actual which constitutes the impasse of the earlier novel; only here, heroic passivity craving beauty and goodness confronts the forces of unappeasable struggle in a closure that endorses the separation of inner and outer worlds.

If Casti represents the novelist's regret, Waymark symbolises his desire. Waymark can be seen to embody the polemical spirit of *Workers in the Dawn* in the process of being overtaken by those elements of Schopenhauerian detachment that direct the description of slum life in *The Unclassed*. His final avowal of 'art for art's sake', for instance, is echoed in Gissing's letters of the time,[3] and in his essay 'The Hope of Pessimism' written in 1882.[4] 'There was a time', Waymark announces, 'when I might have written . . . with a declared social object. That is all gone by. I have no longer any spark of social enthusiasm. Art is all I now care for, and as art I wish my work to be judged' (XXV). Waymark's Paterian affirmation emerges out of the failure of his Hogarthian novel and his challenge to convention. Indeed, though he considers himself and Casti to be artistically opposed, he does not in fact challenge Casti's transcendental division of culture and circumstance. He merely displays a clearer recognition of art's material dependence:

'What can claim precedence, in all this world, over hard cash? It is the fruitful soil wherein is nourished the root of the tree of life; it is the vivifying principle of human activity. Upon

it luxuriate art, letters, science; rob them of its sustenance, and
they droop like withering leaves.'   (VII, 53)

Culture may depend on money and leisure, but for Waymark it
remains mystified. It is for this reason that he can celebrate Casti's
poetry as a true creativity to which the times are unreceptive.
His recognition of the material basis of culture directs him not
to oppose the system that monopolises it, but to join it: 'I was
bent on an intellectual life, forsooth; couldn't see that the natural
order of things was to make money first and be intellectual
afterwards' (VII).

It is this awareness of the importance of wealth in sustaining
culture and self-esteem which also checks Waymark's Romantic
endorsement of passion and individuality in his love-affair with
Ida. Ida's confession on the beach at Hastings is a testimony
to the survival of the pure mind in corrupting circumstance.
The reason Waymark gives for rejecting her is his 'miserable
poverty'. Money – in Gissing, always closely synonymous with
social privilege – alone provides the assurance necessary to transgress the social code. The terms of his refusal initiate a cycle
of humiliation that sets them at enmity, for Ida's scorn in turn
humiliates him by unmasking the final hypocrisy and conventionality of his Bohemian ideals.

There is in fact a certain rift here on the surface of the text. On
the one hand, the novel wants to maintain the purity of Ida's inner
self over external circumstance; on the other hand, it indicates the
inseparability of inner and outer worlds. Money and social position alone are offered as a solution to the loss of self-esteem, and to
the insecurity that attends the transgression of social convention.
It is here that we approach the real personal and social dilemma
which the novel attempts to resolve. Although Gissing declares
that by 'unclassed' he does not mean 'a condition technically
represented by the heroine',[5] the condition of the prostitute is one
with which Gissing's 'unclassed' hero can identify; for the prostitute must bear the humiliation that comes from the discrepancy
between a sense of inner worth and social exclusion. She is thus
a symbol of the division of inner and outer self. Ida's shame does
not derive from the experiences of her past life – her inner self
has, after all, remained inviolate. It derives from the disaccord
between her inner sense of worth and society's judgement. It is a
social injury that demands society's absolution. Her swim in the

sea at midnight is presented with all the symbolism of a ritual purification, and is followed by her withdrawal to a life of hardship and atonement. But Ida lives in a society which provides no ritual solution to the problem of injured dignity. Her return to her job at the laundry; her love of cleanliness: these are given symbolic suggestion, but they cannot remove the chains of her humiliation.

It is at this point that the novel sets in motion a fictional resolution of the internalised social problem presented in Waymark's relationship with Ida – the problem of his Bohemian desire for passion, and his conventional need for integration. It is a dilemma which Waymark himself defensively misrepresents as the conflict between his desire for the unconventional, and Ida's wish for respectability (XXI). In fact, the real crisis is never resolved, but avoided. Waymark's response to the news that Ida has been imprisoned for theft is one of partial relief that 'a position of affairs which had become intolerable was got rid of without his own exertion' (XXIV). The author himself may miss the irony of this; the reader should not. The trial itself clearly marks a retreat from the unresolved social dilemma facing the hero. It is an event which aims to confirm Ida's moral superiority to society's judgement. Like the conventional use of illness in, say, Jane Austen's *Sense and Sensibility*, Ida's imprisonment has the dimensions of a ritual atonement. Significantly it coincides with her grandfather's preparations for her readmission to the 'bourgeois' world.

The movement of the narrative to this end is delayed, however, by the exploration of the hero's ideal of marriage to 'a refined and virtuous woman'. If Waymarks's involvement with Ida demonstrates the fragility of the inner self, his relationship with Maud exposes the inadequacy of conventionality, duty and traditional faith. Waymark aims, in Arnoldian terms, to 'Hellenize' her unsweetened and unenlightened 'Hebraism'; in actual terms, to unite respectability and its social advantages with the assertion of transcendant culture. Maud escapes for a time from her sense of sin on the wings of a Pre-Raphaelite aestheticism, but her encounter with violence and misery in the streets destroys her faith in 'Beauty' as a solace of life, just as her discovery of her mother's sordid liaisons mocks the doctrine of love as the end of being. Maud reverts in the end to the emotional burden of her *de contemptu mundi* faith. It is a spiritual yoke which Waymark defines in terms of the Hebraic-Christian allegory of sin. He himself opposes this with the Hellenic myth of Prometheus in which man saves himself 'not by renunciation, but by the prowess of Hercules, that is to say, the triumphant aspiration of humanity' (XXVII). Yet the novel presents Waymark as marooned between the two, between Maud and Ida, renunciation and aspiration:

'I have in me the elements of an enthusiast; they might have led me to strange developments, but for that cold, critical spirit which makes me so intensely self-conscious. This restless scepticism has often been to me a torment in something the same way as that burden of which you speak.'   (XXVII, 225)

It is here, in Waymark's identification of Maud's burden of sin with his own disabling scepticism and passivity, that we again approach the partially articulated conflict at the novel's core. For sin and the need for atonement are here displayed in a nakedly secular guise. Waymark's desire to enjoy life's fruits is thwarted not only by circumstance, but by the misgiving that attends the disparity between inner ideal and actuality. His social *malaise* arises in part from the clash between his inner sense of worth and his social anonymity. He feels shame for a condition for which he believes he is not responsible, yet which needs atonement.

In respect of his specifically intellectual stature, Waymark also represents the problem of reconciling corporate and individual demands in the new secular, 'bourgeois' state, of squaring the need for authority with the reality of his own social exclusion. Waymark's conflict of radical and conservative sentiment, his claim to spiritual authority from a position of social marginality, finally mark his protest as 'petty bourgeois'. He represents what Terry Eagleton in another context has characterised as the 'impotent idealist conscience' of capitalism.[6] His work as a rent collector – undertaken significantly to support his aesthetic project of writing a Hogarthian novel – unconsciously demonstrates the final complicity of his claim to spiritual authority. He functions as a go-between, serving the capitalist Woodstock, yet meliorating the social misery capitalism creates with a programme of whitewash and fresh draining. It is a role which provides the novel with a symbol of his atonement, both for the burden of challenging the securities of social order, and for the guilt of human betrayal. In the account of his vigil tied to the floor of Slimy's slum (XXVIII), the novel provides a final Christ-like image of suffering and expiation that coincides with Ida's release from prison. Freedom comes to both. The cancellations that take place within the novel once the inheritance code has been invoked in Ida's favour leave the hero, Waymark, in possession of his ideal – inner culture transcending circumstance, yet now granted social sovereignty.

And yet their apotheosis is not immediate. In its account of Casti's Keatsian death on the Isle of Wight and Maud's psychological disablement in the morality of sacrifice, the novel appears to endorse Woodstock's Social Darwinian view that 'it's nature that the strong should rule over the weak' (XVI). Yet if the survival of the fittest is sanctioned as the law of society, the shadow of democratic disorder remains. For Slimy, as well as for the novel's hero, money means happiness. The final propitiations must be made. Ida's active philanthropy, her garden parties for the children of the poor, with their recipe of 'Punch and Judy' and hot water and soap, provide a Dickensian solution to social evil and unrest. The slums are in fact allowed their revenge, but the smallpox which rages there strikes down only the guilty capitalist Woodstock, leaving Ida and Waymark in possession of the future.[7] Their marriage enacts a petty-bourgeois dream in which individuality triumphs over circumstance, and the novel's hero gains privilege and wealth without guilt. Through the restoration of the 'natural' order which is understood to have preceded the narrative – Waymark, we have been told at the beginning of the novel, is really the son of a ruined stockbroker; Ida the granddaughter of the capitalist Woodstock – the social and psychological condition of 'unclassment' is exorcised. The exiles enter their kingdom.

II   PRISONERS OF FICTION: *ISABEL CLARENDON*

Isabel Clarendon (1886) is a novel of ideas in which the intellectual hero is presented for the first time in Gissing's work, not as disinherited or *déclassé*, but as a distinctively male version of Charlotte Brontë's cultured, 'petty-bourgeois' protagonists. One interesting consequence of this arrangement in *Isabel Clarendon* is the prominence given to the problem of the hero's social inferiority to the refined woman with whom he falls in love. It is a situation which prevents a romantic resolution of the conflicts of lower-class aspiration in the convention of hypergamy which Ian Watt has identified as a characteristic feature of the English novel.[8] In this, Gissing's novel clearly has links with Hardy's *The Woodlanders*, published the following year, and with other key fictions of the later Victorian period. The novel's unhappy ending is to some extent the consequence of a refusal to transgress the conventions of the sexual code which forbid a woman to marry beneath her.[9]

It is the novel's inconclusive ending, its refusal to leave behind it 'a sense of imaginative satisfaction' which struck early reviewers and evoked comparisons with Henry James.[10] Yet that this disappointment of 'imaginative satisfaction' reaches even deeper than the unhappy ending is evident in the sense of superiority and occasional bewilderment felt by contemporary reviewers and later critics towards a hero variously described as abnormal, morbid and woefully feeble. What this would seem to indicate is the degree to which the hero's final renunciation of the world is denied the kind of spiritual authority generally granted it within the pattern of the *Bildungsroman* to which the novel would seem to adhere – a pattern which tends to endorse the hero's superiority to the world even in the representation of his inevitable defeat.[11] If *Isabel Clarendon* fails to provide such imaginary supersession, it is because the very terms of its ironic privilege involve a return to those wholly illusory ideals whose mystifications the novel itself has exposed – in *Isabel Clarendon*, a combination of rural radicalism, female beauty worship and Paterian aestheticism. Yet the effect as we read is not simply of illusion turning into reality in a way that exposes Gissing's essential pessimism and conservatism. Such a view tempts John Goode, for example, to class the novel as 'an updated version of the romantic "confession" . . . a kind of *Werther*' which provides 'a valuable guide to Gissing's thinking in the 'eighties'.[12] Rather, the novel disturbingly confronts the absence of intellectual autonomy at the heart of English life in a way that makes visible its hidden traumas and contradictions.

It is revealing in this context to consider Turgenev's influence on *Isabel Clarendon*, which was openly acknowledged by Gissing[13] and which has been made the basis of some critical attention.[14] It is clear that Turgenev had an important influence on Gissing's work as a whole; yet the debt to Turgenev was never simply a superficial matter of setting or character – the relationship of Kingcote and Isabel as an echo of Bazarov's relationship with Anna Sergeyevna, for instance, or Kingcote's resemblance to Rudin. The true significance of that debt lies in the creation of representative characters as bearers of topical ideological forces at work in society – a method of showing character which Dostoevsky was to make the basis of his 'realism in the highest sense'. Character in these terms is not reducible to a merely empirical or psychological reality; nor is it to be viewed allegorically as a mere personification or idea; rather, it has an almost figural quality in which psychology and individual action are seen as manifestations of society's hidden laws. It is this method, together with a preponderance of intellectual types, which gives Gissing's work its strangely European quality. Yet the specific form of that figuration in *Isabel Clarendon* – in particular, the novel's regression to demonstrably anachronistic ideals – is warning against superficial comparisons which obscure the peculiarly English nature of Gissing's work.

Isabel Clarendon expresses an attachment to the ideal of an organic pre-industrial England which Gissing inherited from Carlyle and the nineteenth-century social critics. This retrospective rural radicalism, with its ideal of a functional aristocracy directing a cohesive and hierarchical class structure, does in fact go much further back. It is to be found in the neo-Classical celebration of the 'great house' in Pope's *Moral Essays*, for instance, or a century earlier in Jonson's 'To Penshurst'. Culture, seen as 'a whole way of life', functions in all these instances as a critical category. In the poetry of Jonson and Pope, the ideal of the country house as a seat of civilised life merges with a traditional pastoral critique of the cultural debasement and lack of cohesion of urban life. In the writings of the nineteenth-century social critics, the idealisation of the organic life of the Middle Ages is directed in a similar manner against industrialism and *laissez-faire*. Yet in nineteenth-century England, as Raymond Williams has argued, this critical idea is riven by an abstract and contradictory conception of culture as a 'separate entity' from society.[15] In the neo-Classical ideal the aesthetic component of culture remains firmly lodged in the whole way of life, supporting aristocracy, patronage and the 'great house'. In the writings of nineteenth-century intellectuals, it shifts from an affiliation with a social class to a devotion to beauty and personal feeling opposed to society and the demands of the market. Culture as a critical idea comes to engage a contemporary ideal of a pre-industrial past, and at the same time an essentially ahistorical devotion to art.

The pitfalls of rural-intellectual radicalism as a critique of industrial society are, as Williams argues, the indifference and reactionary idealisation which emerge when retrospective radicalism is made to carry humane feelings and yet ordinarily attach them to a pre-capitalist and therefore irrecoverable world. A necessary social criticism is then directed to the safer world of the past; to a world of books and memories, in which the scholar can be professionally humane but in his own real world either insulated or indifferent.[16]

The focus of the argument is not on whether rural-intellectual radicalism is a genuine critique of industrial capitalism; rather it is on interrogating the consequences when this critique of the present 'must choose its bearings, between past and future'. In *Isabel Clarendon* Bernard Kingcote not only chooses the past, but imagines he find it undisturbed.

In some respects Gissing's hero does in fact resemble Goethe's Werther. Winstoke, like Werther's Wahlheim, is a rural retreat from the corruptions of city life. Here Kingcote finds solace talking to the peasants, the 'worthy clodhoppers' who are as happy as oxen, since they lack imagination and 'townish radicalism' (I.ix). The novel's own account of Winstoke is by contrast hedged round with a sense of reality. Kingcote's cottage is a damp, unhealthy place, and the world which he enters has not after all been immune to industrialism and external change, but has seen the passing of silk manufacture.

This demystification of the naïve hero's poetic view of rural life also applies to the legend of 'The Knight's Well'. The legend provides an ironic focus on the hero's idealisation of the great house and its mistress. It also serves as an anti-realist element, a symbolic device prefiguring Kingcote's fate. Isabel Clarendon, the mistress of Knightswell, is not Kingcote's Petrarchan lady but the daughter of a country solicitor who has managed to escape the 'social limbo' by a fortunate marriage. Clarendon himself is a 'novus homo' from the commercial classes, and one of a long line of 'inglorious' tenants of Knightswell. The unfolding pattern of the narrative is one in which the protagonist moves towards a knowledge which the novelist and the reader have shared all along. The novel can be seen to conform from this point of view to the pattern of the *Bildungsroman*, which ends with the hero's abandonment of his search while still refusing the world of convention. In fact the relationship between the ideal and the actual is more impassible than this reading would allow. Kingcote's ideal serves as a critical focus on the superficial world of Knightswell, but in the end it is the ideal which is shown to be illusory, and what is more, an imaginary distortion of the real relations of existence. It is not simply a question of disappointment, of Kingcote's ideal confronting the actuality of a Knightswell inhabited by a sham grande bourgeoisie and parvenues from the commercial classes. There is a recognition that the very means by which he attempts to negotiate, and finally refuses that degradation is itself the fiction and illusion which supports it.

The novel's subversion of its own moral centre is also evident in its rendering of the Romantic notion of literature itself as a means to a higher reality and truth. All the characters define themselves and are defined in relation to literature. One of the novel's key dichotomies, for instance, is the opposition between the gregarious, anti-intellectual concerns of high society and the moral earnestness of the petty bourgeoisie. To the former belong Isabel and her suitor, Robert Asquith; to the latter, Kingcote and Mr Vission, the country parson who impoverishes himself by subscriptions to literary societies. The novel also represents the world of literary London in the character of Kingcote's friend, Thomas Meres. To the extent that his literary attachments remain uncontaminated by commerce, Kingcote tends ultimately to be treated as more exclusively cultured and humane. The initial contrast, however, is between the antiquarianism of Kingcote and the anti-intellectualism of Asquith. If Asquith is capable of looking ironically on the 'social economy' of the *décolleté* costume, he nevertheless remains like Isabel within a world which prefers Marryat or the newspapers to George Eliot.

It is the novel's claims for the moralising and humanising effects of literature which underlie its central structuring metaphor of 'society as a stage'. It is a motif which arises in part from the Romantic tradition that the material world is illusion, and only the spiritual world has reality. Here the vision of life as a series of roles is one which supports Kingcote's refusal to 'play the walking gentleman' (I.x). Isabel for instance, objects to Rhoda Meres, the daughter of an impoverished literary man, going on stage because 'ladies don't do such things' (III.iii). She dismisses the stage as a place for the 'unsuccessful ones' who have 'lost their place in society'; but in expressing a conventional view, she appears to miss the ironic light it throws on her own position.

A consciousness of this irony emerges in her relationship with her ward, Ada Warren. Ada, who is Clarendon's illegitimate daughter, is the living accusation of the 'refined insincerity' of her marriage without love:

> 'That I should take the child and rear it to inherit his property, or else lose everything at once. With a woman of self-respect, such a scheme would have been empty; she would have turned away in scorn. But he knew me well; he knew . . . that I would rather suffer through years, be the talk and pity and contempt of everyone, face at last the confession to her, – all that rather than be poor again!'   (I.xiii, 283-4)

Her punishment lies in the awareness of her dependence on material things, a dependence which threatens her conception of her ideal self. This wound is opened by the appearance of Lacour. To Isabel his attentions to Ada are merely those of a fortune-hunter, but the fortune he seeks is the one she herself sought to win in the same marriage market.

Lacour also considers going on stage (I.v). His theatre, however, remains society itself. One of the striking features of the novel's characterisation is that Lacour remains in many ways an attractive, even a sympathetic figure in spite of his unattractive qualities. The novel attaches no blame to his selfish calculations. Its ironic view of Lacour's heartless manoeuvres is directed not against his insincerity as such; rather, it demonstrates the disparity between self-justification and motivation. The shift is from man as an 'essence' to man as an 'actor'. Even Lacour's confession that he is a 'frank egoist' and thus 'of necessity sincere' is shown to be directed as much by the forces of egoism and self-idealisation – by the need to secure his own identity – as to the attainment of specific ends. Man's actions and words are seen to involve a calculation of effects whose roots lie nevertheless beyond conscious intention; all finally situate the individuals as a 'subject' within a way of seeing opposed to the realities of existence. Yet in the end this is no less true of Kingcote, who refuses 'the theatre of the world' in his search for, and assertion of his essential self. His literary aestheticism also breeds distortions of reality and disembodied ideals. His existential denial of 'identity' and the past is in the end merely a rejection of his social origins in a traditional class-conscious society in which the conflicting doctrine of individualism has nevertheless taken root.

The frailty of the hero's position is especially evident in his separation of town and country life. Admittedly, there is a palpable lack of irony in the account of Kingcote's return to London which would seem to endorse his contrast between the hideous welter of the town and the tranquillity and spiritual obligations of the country (II.iv). Yet the hero's question, 'Was *that* a dream of joy, or *this* a hideous vision?', is not simply rhetorical. In a sense they are both dreams, both literary versions of the world. Kingcote's London with its rush and welter and predatory relations is no less fictional than his pastoral ideal. Both are shaped in the enduring tradition of 'town and country' fiction which, in exposing urban evils, disguises the homologous relations of oppression uniting both worlds. Isabel's London after all is the world of the 'season' in which the city traditionally serves the ruling class as marriage and business market, as well as social distraction. It is from the polite and flippant world of the 'season' that Kingcote turns away in horror, seeking to free the essential Isabel from its artificialities. He finally recognises, however, not only the impossibility of abstracting Isabel from her social milieu, but the interdependence of town and country life in terms of class and social relations. It is not that Kingcote's ideal of refinement and cultured sensitivity does not exist, an ideal criticising the atomism of urban industrial life. The final irony is that its very existence is seen to depend on the support and ordering of that very society. It is this which pinpoints the illusory nature of Kingcote's ideal. Isabel's sincerity is not a sham; nor is it the 'selfish calculation' of a conscious hypocrite. It is a virtue of character which depends on the social and material advantages she has won from life.

This in a sense is what Ada Warren 'knows'. Ada is the novel's internal dramatic perspective on Kingcote's ideals. She is the enigma that confronts him, the bearer of the secret he will possess at the close. It is Ada who first mocks the antiquarian tendencies of Kingcote's literary cultivation:

> Isabel presented him to Miss Warren, then took the volume from his hands and looked into it.
> 'You know Sir Thomas Browne, no doubt, Ada,' she said.
> 'I know the 'Urn-burial', Ada replied, calmly examining the visitor.   (I.vi, 121)

On one level Ada's intellectual resistance to society and its forms refuses that identification of the conventional with the natural which is the basis of Isabel's 'practical virtues'. Yet on another level – and this is one of the most interesting features of *Isabel Clarendon* – Ada's refusal also stems from her sense that femininity itself is a 'fiction'.

Plain, bookish, indifferent to compliments: Ada's 'masculine' characteristics repel and unnerve Kingcote. Later he will discover that she represents a truer, more authentic type of woman than either his own hopelessly fictional ideal of 'the fair, sweet, queenly woman', or the collusive, pragmatic, wholly feminine Isabel. Ada's final renunciation of society and the country house is not only a political rejection of a world that is no longer the genuine centre of wider social and moral values; it is also a refusal of woman's dependent and parasitical status in that world. Unable to silence her inward ironic voice, unwilling to accept the humiliating self-suppression and denial of identity that the conventions of the sexual code would seem to dictate, Ada heralds the emergence in Gissing's fiction of the image of those 'hybrids' or 'men-women' caricatured by journalists and ardent anti-feminists of the period.[17] This is not to suggest that Ada is in any sense a militant separatist. Her desire for a man's love and her burning 'Who am I?' indicate her innermost sense of lack, insignificance, supplementarity. Her childhood has significantly been overshadowed by an absent father, a deficit which may be seen to have left unresolved or undecided that moment of 'castration' and repression of phallic sexuality which one has come to identify, since Freud, as the symbolic, ideological, psychoanalytic basis of female sexuality.[18] Yet Ada does not simply serve the novel as an image of unfulfilled and incomplete womanhood. Isabel's 'Poor Ada!' may denote the world's condescending, disingenuous pity for what is seen to be Ada's repulsive, jarring sexlessness, but it also expresses a fear of one who resists incorporation within the symbolic securities of gender. The radical primacy of woman's bisexual nature which feminist theorists have deconstructed in the psychoanalytic writings of Freud[19] is here fictionally prefigured in the suspended, undecided sexuality of Ada Warren. In choosing Chelsea rather than Knightswell, struggle rather than ornamental womanhood, Ada represents the possibility of a new type of woman – one who refuses to accept her incompleteness, and who asserts with heroism her 'double' undecidable self.

It is here, however, in its very gestures of radical 'otherness', that the novel lays bare the strangely disabling nature of its own perspectives. For in the contrasting attitudes of Ada and Kingcote to their 'superfluousness', Gissing gives a particularly English direction to the two oppositional tendencies of the intelligentsia in the nineteenth century, idealism and nihilism, vividly depicted in the novels of Turgenev and Dostoevsky. Ada in this context is clearly the anti-idealist voice in the novel, the 'atheist' and new intellectual type who ridicules Kingcote's reverence for the old order. Yet in choosing a literary career in London, Ada ultimately confines her energies to an aesthetic realm of ideology that cannot fundamentally challenge the existing structure of English class formations. This in the end is what Kingcote 'knows'. If Kingcote finally refuses Chelsea, it is because he recognises the ultimately marginal nature of Bohemia and its ideological dependence on the very society to which it represents a reaction.

In examining *Isabel Clarendon*, we have traced a disjunction in the narrative. One the one hand there is an attempt in the novel to grant moral privilege to the idealistic hero. The ironic opposition of 'culture' and 'refinement', for instance, is clearly in accord with the hero's faith in the humanising influence of literature. Yet Kingcote's discourse, in particular his finally bombastic parody of Shakespearian passion (I.xiii) and medieval *fin amour* (II.iii), is allowed no ultimate authority among the plurality of competing discourses generated by the novel's literary motifs. It is revealing in this context that Gissing should have begun to read devoutly through Dante's *Divina Commedia* during the writing of *Isabel Clarendon*.[20] The influence of Gissing's rapturous reading of Dante is evident both in Kingcote's idealisation of Isabel, and in the authority the novel arrogates to itself in supporting the hero's poetic or metaphorical response to the world. Of Dante's Beatrice, Gabriel Josipovici has written that

> She is not a personification but a real person . . . Dante's whole effort is directed at making us accept her as such; it is because she is both real *and* a miracle that she is important to him, for it is this double fact that guarantees the meaningfulness of the universe and God's divine plan.[21]

In *Isabel Clarendon* too, the heroine is both a 'real' person and a miracle. Here, however, we find ourselves in a purely rhetorical world in which the hero's poetic response to the world has no final validity or truth. Indeed it is the novel's attempt to uphold the hero's subjective and finally metaphorical view of Isabel Clarendon which serves to undermine its claim to replace falsifying imagination with the 'true' meaning to which the reader, in a position of tragic foreknowledge, has already been directed.

This disturbance is particularly marked in the novel's denouement. One one level Kingcote's renunciation of Isabel, like Ada's refusal of her legacy, is clearly meant to assert a moral superiority over 'the choice of lower things'. His sacrifice and self-denial, like the suicide of Goethe's Werther, become a reproach to the world and mark a heroic preservation of an ideal he has failed inevitably and tragically to realise. Yet this refusal serves paradoxically to conserve Kingcote's already demystified ideal of Isabel herself. The novel recognises the dependence of that ideal on a precise ordering of social conditions; but it does so not in order to dispense with the opposition of the ideal and the actual; instead, it would seem to hold them more firmly against each other in order to endorse Kingcote's ideal of Isabel's 'spiritual beauty' in the face of degrading circumstance.

Yet Kingcote fails in the end not because Isabel is unwilling to renounce her world, but because he himself refuses her sacrifice and reproach:

> Imagine this woman some day cooling in her love, and speaking with her pale face unutterable things. She would have a right to reproach him, and a reproach divined would drive him to frenzy.   (II.iii, 79)

His refusal of her contractual sacrifice is ultimately a recognition of the material dependence of his ideal, and the real social and sexual conditions of the times. The fate of his sister who has married beneath her is a cautionary reminder of the sacrifice he demands of Isabel. If Gissing does not resort to the solution adopted by George Eliot in *Felix Holt*, it is because he cannot elevate individual morality over a consciousness of material and social constraint. One of the interesting aspects of the novel's ending is the degree to which it exposes the absence of an autonomous place or function for the emergent intellectual such as Kingcote in the advancing industrial world of late-nineteenth-century England. All that is left him is the marginality of a radical conservative or liberal humanist morality in which he is doomed ultimately to serve the dominant class that excludes him. What we are directed to in the end, and what this reading has tried to emphasise, is not what the novel might urge us to believe, but what it is forced to recognise as it attempts to resolve the conflicts between its ideological dream and the encompassing realities of society to which the fiction itself would finally refer.

III   THE EROTIC MARTYRDOM OF EMILY HOOD: *A LIFE'S MORNING*

It is generally recognised that the plot of *A Life's Morning* (1888) owes a great deal to Charlotte Brontë.[22] The novel embodies a conflict between passion and conscience in which passion corresponds to the heroine's desire for elevation into the world to which she feels she belongs by right of nature; and conscience, to a personal inviolability in the face of social disadvantage. The movement in *Jane Eyre*, for example, is towards elevation through the harmonising of these conflicting aspects of 'intellectual egoism'. *A Life's Morning* repeats this central movement, but it does so in a way that completely transforms the issue involved.

The difference is perhaps best seen in the novel's dual structure which undoubtedly confused contemporary reviewers. In general they tended to identify Wilfred Athel as the novel's hero, though, like the reviewer of the London *Guardian*,[23] many were uneasy about Athel's heroic claims. The drama which opens the narrative engages at one level an educational issue. It is the conflict between Athel's positivistic approach to knowledge, and Emily's self-cultivation through the 'literature of Beauty'. Athel characterises himself as 'a one-sided academical monster' for whom the pursuit of rational certainties, the 'knowledge of books', has given way to the cultivation of feelings and 'knowledge of a deeper kind'. In this sense, Athel's collapse and recovery closely parallel the situation described by J. S. Mill in his *Autobiography*.

The triangle which places Athel between Beatrice Redwing and Emily also represents a related conflict between conventionality and an inward ethical demand. This pattern repeats in part Waymark's choice between Ida Starr and Maud Enderby in *The Unclassed*; but whereas for the lower middle-class hero of *The Unclassed* the choice between the conventional and the natural engaged a problem of class, for Athel and the 'free' world of the country house, it emerges as a purely private issue. Athel urges Beatrice to surmount the inconsistency and insincerity of a life divided between religiosity and the social masquerade by surrendering to the spirit of the age. This involves self-cultivation through aestheticism and humanistic pursuits:

> 'There is a self in every one of us; the end of our life is to discern it, bring it out, make it actual. You don't yet know your own self; you have not the courage to look into your heart and mind; you keep over your eyes the bondage of dogmas in which you only half believe. . . . Cannot you see that the world has outgrown the possibility of one universal religion? For good or for evil, each of us must find a religion in himself.' (II, 32)

For Athel the pursuit of passion and individuality may encounter social disapproval, but no higher ethical sanction. In the free world of wealth and privilege, aestheticism and respectability sit comfortably together. Athel's choice of Emily, the choice of aestheticism and individuality, is a personal issue in which passion and ethical demand are finally unproblematic. It is within this space that the novel's drama of elevation and transcendence is acted out. At the centre of the novel, however, is Emily herself for whom passion and duty are elements of a fierce internalised class conflict.

The conflict here is between the freedom of the country house and the psychological and material oppressions of 'home'. Emily manifests the 'deliberate reticence' and 'extreme moderation' characteristic of Charlotte Bronte's heroines. This is explained as her 'concession to the fate which had made her a governess', and paradoxically as her means of exercising power over 'those whose bread she ate' (III). It is the force of her individuality betraying itself 'even under the disadvantage of complete self-suppression' which at first attracts Wilfred Athel. Yet if for Jane Eyre the obstacle to passion is a fierce ethical demand ambiguously rooted in the need for social as well as personal elevation, for Emily Hood this demand is seen by contrast to derive not from individualism or personal judgement, but from involuntary social attachment. It is not so much that Emily sacrifices her happiness 'in the name of an austere personal morality,[24] but rather that the sense of betrayal that attends her social and intellectual elevation sets in motion a psychological mechanism of guilt and sacrificial atonement.

The relationship between culture and sensibility here constitutes the novel's problematic centre. Emily's humble life is
offered as an illustration of the inner dissolution which attends
'that intellectual egoism which is the note of our time' (V).
Her response to the conflict between her 'religion of beauty'
and the pull towards sympathy and sacrifice is to retreat to
'the sheltered purity of her own heart' (VII). The anecdote
of Emily's childhood sacrifice for the dog by the roadside
is offered as the origin of that dread of compassionateness
which she later feels towards her father and the world of home:

> the haggard gaze of fate should not daunt one; pity is but
> an element in the soul's ideal of order, it should not usurp
> a barren sovereignty. It is the miserable contradiction of our
> lot that the efficiency of the instincts of beauty-worship waits
> upon a force of individuality attainable only by a sacrifice of
> sensibility. Emily divined this. So it was that she came to shun
> the thought of struggle, to seek an abode apart from turbid
> conditions of life. She was hard at work building for her
> soul its 'lordly pleasure-house', its Palace of Art.   (V, 69-70)

Emily's Paterian folding together of art and life in a fierce, cold
chastity is her solution to the conflict of culture and sensibility.
It marks a refusal of the disabling pity of the weak-victim man
such as her father who is unable 'to feel unkind even to
a town' (V). Yet as the novel shows, this rejection of pity
cannot free Emily from her attachments. Rather, it becomes the
psychological spring of her entrapment and final exile.

One of the striking aspects of the novel is its recognition of
the psychological as well as external traps that lie in wait for the
individual in the new industrial order. Paradoxically this finally
supports an overarching mystification in which the enlightened
grand-bourgeois world of the Baxendales and the Athels is seen to
exist outside the inhumane system presided over by the mill-owner
and capitalist, Dagworthy. The isolation of the old humanitarian
order from capitalism is historically false and misleading, and yet
it plainly corresponds to the *apparent* conditions of existence in
the free consumptional world of the country house. On the
positive side, the novel shows both capitalist and worker, master
and man, enchained together in the same psychological snares

of an inhumane system. The analogy which links the hungry dog to the roadside with Emily's father is extended to include the employer of labour, the 'hunger god' himself, first showing his chained dogs (V), and later 'like a beaten dog' before Emily (X). In setting a trap for her, Dagworthy is himself entrapped by frustrated desires which have been perverted to instincts of accumulation in one who 'represented an intermediate stage of development between the hard-headed operative who conquers wealth, and his descendants who shall know what use to make of it' (VIII).

One of the implicit correspondences that emerges from Emily's encounter with Dagworthy is the parallel between his refusal of feeling and her resistance to pity. If feeling for Dagworthy is destructive of his resolve (X), pity for Emily is destructive of her 'Palace of Art' (XI). Both are ensnared in an inhumane order in which desire attaches itself to the free personality whose foundations are in separation rather than in social relation. For Dagworthy the appropriation of value can only express itself in the mentality of ownership and domination, of 'having', which would reduce Emily to an object. Yet Emily's own desire and resistance in turn can only express themselves in a self-regarding aestheticism that fixes the self as a precious commodity. In Emily's case the conflict between education and solidarity finds a parallel in Hardy's *The Return of the Native*, but whereas Clym Yeobright chooses to raise the class at the expense of the individual, Emily Hood chooses individuality at the expense of the class. Both paths lead equally to entrapment. The force of circumstance cannot be overcome within an idealist conscience. Emily resists external forces only to fall into the chains of an internalised social conflict.

In her attempt to transcend her social origins, Emily is taken on a 'guilt-trip'. In refusing the contractual love that belongs properly to community and fraternity, she invokes the example of Isabella's 'passion for purity' in *Measure for Measure*. Betrayal is chosen in the knowledge that the sacrifice she has been asked to make is 'disproportionate to the disaster threatened' (XII). This is of course perfectly true, and the story must be said to suffer accordingly; but this is clearly not the point. The Oedipal drama at the centre of the novel is nakedly symbolic. It is the concrete rendering of the tensions of the upward-striving individual in a class-stratified society which has given itself over to individualistic doctrines and post-Enlightenment beliefs in man's essential nature. Here the literary reference finally measures a distance rather than enforces a comparison. In *Measure for Measure* the metaphysical sovereignty of justice and the 'Soul' remains absolute in spite of the secular challenge to theological rigidity. In the pervasively secular world of *A Life's Morning*, idealistic specialisation of virginity and individual conscience has no metaphysical foundation or absolute sanction over social bondage and material needs.

Emily's renunciation of passion and social elevation in the wake of her father's death answers in Freudian terms to a double need – to the need to preserve her 'forbidden wish', and the need for this wish to be punished.[25] The first unites, in Emily's image of Athel and the country house, all that connects with the highest in human nature – Emily's aesthetic, her moral and her cultural goals, as well as her social aspirations and drives towards self-assertion. Emily's 'ego-ideal' is in this sense her father's wish. She is the recipient of his failed aspirations and thwarted hopes. This is the bond between them. He has tied himself to the capitalist's mill, choosing to subordinate and sacrifice himself to secure her education, and ultimately in awe of her 'mental and moral independence' (IX). Yet Emily's ego-ideal has its shadow in the sense of injustice and pity with which she regards her father's passivity and sacrifice. The conflict of Emily's nature is, in the language of the novel, between 'culture' and 'sensibility', in which the former corresponds to her ego-ideal, and the latter to her sense of injustice and ultimately of guilt.

It is significant that at the moment of her renunciation these two conflicting sides of her nature are described in the sado-masochistic image of martyrdom:

> What was her first sensation, when the door had closed, then the gate without, and Wilfred in very deed was gone? Was it hopeless misery, failure, dread foresight of the life she still must live? Rather her mood was that of the martyr who has held firm to the last wrench of torture, who feels that agony is overcome and fear of self surpassed. This possibility had there ever been in Emily, though associating with such variant instincts. Circumstances had brought the occasion which weighed one part of her nature against the other, and with this result. (XVI, 237)

That this possibility had 'ever been in Emily' indicates that her chosen martyrdom is a symptom of a psychological compulsion rather than a response to an arbitrary event. Emily's renunciation is a symptomatic regression to 'moral masochism', to the need for 'sin' and punishment, in which unsublimated desires are turned inwards against the self. In this sense the novel's central drama is an external rendering of Emily's inner condition, of the 'trouble' evoked by Athel's suggestion that a case might arise which would call upon her to make some sacrifice on her father's behalf (I). Masochism, as Freud argues, 'regularly occurs where a cultural suppression of the instincts holds back a large part of the subject's destructive instinctual components from being exercised in life'.[26]

One of the notable features of Emily's social and cultural aspiration is her fierce self-suppression in the Athel household. It takes the form of a compensatory cult of beauty, a Paterian fantasy of contemplative detachment from the material conditions of existence. It answers to the need to deny the 'wish' which is in a sense *killing her father*, and to the need to deny the 'compassionateness' which would destroy her ideal. Yet, as the central drama shows, this aesthetic specialisation of the self, like her forbidden wish, is answerable to the sanctions of betrayal, responsibility and guilt. Within the specific context of a world of class division and 'meritocracy', Emily stands, as in Freud's own image of man, as a battleground of life and death instincts, trapped within the intolerable choice of either destroying others or destroying herself. Her final renunciation, in which life instincts are turned inwards in an erotic martyrdom, contrives the supreme punishment – faithfulness to her wish and denial of its fulfilment. It is a condition which the novel characterises in its own Romantic, pre-psychoanalytic terminology as 'idealism' charged with 'morbid dominance' (XVI). Emily's sterile asceticism is in the final analysis the resistance of the victim, the self-denial of one who has already been denied.

What is valuable in *A Life's Morning* derives from its ironic supersession of its own idealistic centre. Its perspective, unlike that of *Villette* or *Young Werther*, for instance, in which the ideal survives, however ambiguously, even in defeat, is one of ineluctable materialism which may be abhorred but cannot be refused; which in terms of the novel's symbolic rendering of Emily's internal conflict reaches out to include both inner and outer worlds. This is the point of impasse and irresolution to which Gissing's major novels of the 1890s, such as *New Grub Street* and *Born in Exile*, will come unequivocally to rest. In the three works we have been examining, there is a retreat from this intolerable disclosure to a mythological resolution in the ideological wish. In *The Unclassed* this is achieved by the fairy-tale device of disinheritance. In *Isabel Clarendon* the pattern of the *Bildungsroman* attempts on one level to endorse the moral superiority of the petty-bourgeois hero in a debased world, and to preserve in part the ideal against the recognition of inescapable circumstance that emerges from the novel's demystifying configurations. Here in *A Life's Morning* the retreat from the novel's disclosure involves both structural disjunction and a metonymic displacement from the social to the private.

Mrs Baxendale's view of Emily's renunciation, 'We are not living in a novel; there are no such things as mysteries which last a lifetime' (XVII), contains a double irony. They are characters in a novel, and it is precisely because they are that the mystery to which she refers is open to some form of resolution. Yet these words indicate too a distinction between life itself, in which contradictions may be resolved in the 'lived', and fiction, in which ideology may be thrown into crisis and disarray. The irony here is that what is seen to be the novel's mystery, its enigma awaiting resolution, is in fact its real knowledge. Through its fictional concretisation of the petty-bourgeois crisis of conscience in the world of industrial capitalism, the novel exposes a contradiction between ideology and the real relations of existence which cannot be resolved within the liberal humanist resources of the ideologically given.

The novel's retreat from this disclosure involves a structural shift from the problematic heroine to the free hero whose choice lies between a public and a private life, between society and personal cultivation. The triumph of feeling over thinking which directs the final choices is in fact the force that embraces both Emily's resistance and her psychological injury, but here in the free world of the country house is granted transcendental status. The degree of freedom available in this emotionally charged but unproblematic world is particularly evident, for instance in Beatrice's renunciation of marriage and conventional society for the self-discovery of a singing career: what in Gissing's later novels of the 1890s, such as *The Odd Women* and *The Whirlpool*, will constitute the crisis of female identity and individualism in a patriarchal society, is here presented as a personal and thus a negotiable issue. Through its displacement to the 'personal' the novel enters an area of abstraction which nevertheless exposes its decentred nature. In the shift from heroine to hero, Emily emerges from her purgatorial exile as a pure, noble being, rather than, as the central dilemma suggests, an idealist who embodies in her religion of beauty an internalised class conflict. The Christian purgatorial theme is here invoked to produce a contrived mythological resolution in which, in the realm of the personal, the hero appropriates the individuality and ethical resistance of the petty-bourgeois heroine, and the heroine in turn realises her forbidden wish.

3

Gissing and 'The People'

> *A map of the world which does not include Utopia*
> *is not worth even glancing at, for it leaves out the*
> *one country at which humanity is always landing.*
> Oscar Wilde

I GISSING AND THE INDUSTRIAL NOVEL

The three novels written by Gissing between 1885 and 1888 on 'the condition of the people' – *Demos*, *Thyrza* and *The Nether World* – have always attracted critical attention, if only as successors to the 'industrial novel' of the 1840s and 1850s. *Demos*, as one early reviewer of the novel observed, 'might have been written by the author of *Alton Locke* and of *North and South*, or of *Shirley*'.[1] And yet if Gissing revives many of the recurrent concerns and motifs of the earlier industrial novels, he adds new elements that call for separate critical definition.

Gissing's novels on 'the condition of the people' can in fact be seen as the meeting-point of two distinct traditions – the tradition of the industrial novel with its central conflict of 'labour' and 'capital', set generally in the industrial north; and the Dickensian novel of urban adventure with its vision of human diversity, and its appeal to sympathy in the wider, more perplexing division of rich and poor.[2] What is evident in Gissing's novels is an erosion of those liberal humanist values which in the classic realist novel had provided the basis of a fictional solution to the problem of social injustice and political unrest. In the novels which traditionally constitute the category of 'industrial novel' –

Disraeli's *Sybil* (1845), Mrs Gaskell's *Mary Barton* (1848) and *North and South* (1854), Kingsley's *Alton Locke* (1850), Dickens's *Hard Times* (1854) and George Eliot's later *Felix Holt* (1866) – a liberal humanist emphasis on tolerance and sympathy towards the sufferings and demands of 'labour' answers, in its appeal to the personal, both to the demands of conscience and to the desire to preserve the existing social structure against the challenge of labour solidarity. 'By personalizing class conflict', P. J. Keating writes,

> and placing blame on the human failings of individual employ-
> ers and employees, sympathy is aroused for the workers'
> appalling conditions without this being taken to imply that
> there is anything fundamentally wrong with the social structure
> as a whole.[3]

The appeal to personal reformation provides a viewpoint not only for shifting the blame for social misery from the inhumane system to the faults of individual employers, but also for discrediting all those forms of social protest, such as Chartism, socialism or trade unionism, which emphasise social division. The riot is one of the recurrent motifs of the industrial novel, dramatising middle-class fears of violence, and identifying mass labour consolidation with mob violence.

The appeal to individual reform as a solution to class antago-nism and social injustice produces in these novels a recurrent spectacle of middle-class humanitarianism and working-class atonement. This pattern is reinforced in both *Sybil* and *Felix Holt* by the conventional devices of inheritance and lost wills through which the segregated worlds of the classes are brought into contact. Here again the conflict enters the novel in the form of its resolution, for the conventional motifs involve a return to an overriding moral order. These modes of resolution constitute the dominant structure of the industrial novel from Disraeli to George Eliot. In Dickens's novels of urban adventure there is a similar restoration of the natural, moral order by means of the structure of sentiment and melodrama, although by *Dombey and Son*, as John Lucas has shown, this return has become more prob-lematic, and the tone of the later novels approaches pessimism.[4]

By the 1880s history had intervened to impoverish the conven-tional structure of sentiment and melodrama. It was the reluctant view of one contemporary reviewer, for instance, that Gissing's pessimism, however unpleasant, more nearly reflected the reality of the times that the philanthropic panaceas offered in Walter Besant's popular romances of the East End.[5] Philanthropy itself had come to seem inadequate. It was discredited not only because it was unable to cope with the sheer extent of urban poverty, but because of changes in public opinion. To the rich, charity came to mean mendicity and dissipation; to the poor, the transformation of a natural right into a depersonalised humiliation.[6] At the same time, philanthropy came to be seen as part of a wider problem of urban, specifically London life, which involved the weakening of social cohesion through the geographical zoning of rich and poor. It is in representing the segregated nature of urban life that Gissing links the distinct traditions of the industrial novel and the novel of urban adventure; for the diversity of Dickens's London is dissolved by Gissing in an image of spatial organisation and separation which re-engages, in a new setting, the class antagonisms and threat of 'labour' at the centre of the industrial novel. Gissing's formal strategy in this context is to reverse the conventional, basically Romantic structure of the earlier industrial novel. The conventional themes and motifs of the earlier industrial novel are reintroduced – lost wills and inheritance; inter-class love relationships – but these no longer resolve the threat of class conflict through the restoration of a natural, hierarchical order; rather they expose the unbridgeable gulf between the classes and the idealism of corporate hopes.

The effect of this anti-Romantic structure is on one level deeply contradictory; for in refusing corporate hopes of reform, Gissing produces an image of class conflict that undermines the very basis of his Arnoldian challenge to industrialism and anarchy. Gissing himself is to be understood in this respect as part of that whole process of containment which characterised English society in the latter half of the nineteenth century. As one of the emergent intelligentsia who confronted the problems of industrial democracy during the 1880s, Gissing manifests that peculiarly English, and potentially disabling combination of Arnoldian humanist education and lower-class marginality. It is this specific cultural formation which finally distinguishes his novels on 'the condition of the people' from the earlier industrial novel. At the risk of simplification, one could say that Gissing's opposition to industrial society is cultural rather than moral as in, say, Mrs Gaskell, although behind both oppositions lies a common fear of disorder. Yet if Gissing's cultural critique of industrialism is one which refuses the idealist-interventionist resolutions of social crisis found in the earlier industrial novel, so too is it refused the ultimate authority that attends a modernist extrication or migration from the decisive social world. Culture for Gissing may support the claims of inner autonomy, but from his position of social marginality, it is also identified with the refinement of a higher social stratum. For this reason Gissing is never able to dispense with the decisive community of classic realism. Recognising the inadequacy of liberal humanist values and culture from above as a means of transforming society, Gissing's novels on the condition of the people expose the insupportability of their own cultural reformist project in a way that would seem to threaten their formal coherence.

This discrepancy between an author's aims and the position affirmed by his work is not an uncommon one; it indicates the degree to which literature is never simply an aesthetic expression of the author's position. If that conflict would seem to be exacerbated in Gissing's case, it is because he fails to produce any secure grounds of identification or privilege for the reader, either in the author's interpretations and criticisms or in the 'truth' of the work. This is not to suggest that Gissing's novels fail to achieve a symbolic transcendence or reconciliation of their own internal contradictions. In *Demos*, for instance, the reconciliation of a cultural opposition to industrialism with a fear of anarchy and insurgence is accomplished by a series of distortions and simplifications of the historical conflict the novel claims to depict. By representing the Industrial Revolution as a confrontation between rural aristocracy and an insurgent proletariat, for example, Gissing is able to preserve his Arnoldian ideal of culture in his untainted middle-class characters. In *Thyrza* and *The Nether World*, the fear of democratic unrest is exorcised by a blindness to historical change itself in an imagined image of permanent class difference. In *Thyrza* where the plot still centres on an inter-class love relationship, the preservation of the Arnoldian ideal can only be accomplished by a kind of fiat; in *The Nether World* where the condition of entrapment and alienation among the poor is presented as absolute, the Arnoldian ideal is preserved in the self-exemptions of the authorial voice, which is by turns caustic, cultured, pitying. The problem with these novels in the end is not that they offend against an ideal of the organic form of the novel which Lawrence referred to as the novel's vital or living 'inter-relatedness' in all its parts. If they dissatisfy, it is because the contrivances of their enforced harmonisation are in the end so nakedly visible, since the terms of their reality and 'truth' can only be located in those very forms of moral and literary aestheticism whose inadequacy, as a response to social crisis, the novels themselves have already exposed.

The disturbance in these works to the satisfying collusions between text and reader is undoubtedly damaging from one point of view; yet it is also unquestionably the source of their strange insights. For what is being consistently revealed in these novels is the fragility of that symbolic exemption they would compel us to share. We are forced in effect to consider the nature of those falsifications towards which the pressure of a position resembling that of Gissing might urge us.[7] More positively they reveal the cultural autonomy and necessary resistances of working-class life itself to an incorporation whose ambiguities are all on show. The result is a picture of the urban proletariat which is not simply accommodated to ideals of social harmony and corporate control. This involves a profound understanding on Gissing's part of psychological as well as specifically social constraints – in particular, of the traumas of irrational protest and injured pride in which individuals paradoxically accept the terms of their own subordination. Admittedly there is a comforting pessimism in Gissing's presentation of these constraints; indeed his novels have often been criticised for reflecting the abstract rather than the dynamic aspects of society. Yet this very suspension of the process of social change can also be seen to result in Gissing's unique description of working-class life in Hoxton, Lambeth or Clerkenwell as one of a genuine community with its own cultural network of human relationships, antagonisms and palliatives. Moreover in describing a world where this abstraction of things has become the reality in which men live, Gissing would seem to recognise the degree to which irrational protest aspires to an authentic, if finally self-ruinous basis of autonomy and resistance to the absorptions of reason, utilitarianism and culture from above.

II CULTURE AND CLASS CONFLICT: *DEMOS*

Demos (1886) is undoubtedly the most ambitious of Gissing's early novels. It was also the most popular and commercially successful in its day. Written in response to the deepening social unrest in the early 1880s (Gissing was particularly distressed by the Trafalgar Square Riot of 8 February 1886 which resulted in the arrest of William Morris), *Demos* is a political melodrama which can be compared with Dostoevsky's masterly novel *à thèse*, *The Devils*, in its attempt to render not so much actual historical characters or events, but the compelling ideas at work in the society of his time. The satirical impulse behind both novels is nakedly conservative. One might note that Dostoevsky's scorn is reserved for the intelligentsia, whereas Gissing's satire is directed against 'working class aims and capacities'.[8] Yet the reader is soon aware that what is being revealed in Gissing's novel is not in the end the moral and aesthetic deficiencies of working-class people, but the ideological poverty of the socialist ideal conceived in terms of the specific cultural crisis of the freelance English intellectual in the latter half of the nineteenth century. Specifically *Demos* indicates an unresolved conflict of traditional values and individualistic doctrines which the novel's symbolic resolution in the conventions of hypergamy and inheritance does not finally dispel.

Demos, as John Goode has interestingly suggested, broadly enacts a Comtist historiography with Eldon representing the 'theological' and Mutimer the 'metaphysical' stage of human intellectual development, with the final 'positive' stage failing to realise itself in a moralised capitalism.[9] This conception of the novel, though schematic and tentative, clearly raises to a more generalised level Raymond Williams's view that *Demos* is marked by a shift from hopes of reform to the social and political disillusionments of Gissing's 'negative identification'.[10] In fact positivism is always in Gissing a pre-textual solution, a discredited possibility. Even in *Workers in the Dawn*, the heroine's 'religion of humanity' is the target of irony. Yet the notion implicit in both critics is basically correct – namely that disillusionment is the basis of the narrative's disclosure and the point of ironic supersession of discredited solutions to the cultural crisis of the 1880s. In this broad schematic view of the novel Adela is clearly central. It is she who undergoes the intellectual journey and who emerges transcendent from the fierce negative polemic fabricated at the novel's core.

Adela stands in a sense as an analogue of the valley itself in a process of change from the spiritual order of the old landed aristocracy to the spiritual aridity of disruptive radical programmes.

These are presented as mere rationalisations of egoism in an athe-
istic age. The aristocractic order is already benighted when the
novel opens. The land and power of the Eldons has been absorbed
by Richard Mutimer's great-uncle, an industrialist entrepreneur
who devotes himself to propping up the hereditary status of the
Eldons out of 'native conservatism' and a snobbish reverence
for 'gentility' and 'culture' (III). The actual historical fusion of
aristocratic and bourgeois interests which this betokens – a fusion
whose conditions were in part prepared for by the capitalisation of
land in England during the eighteenth century, and in part by the
inability in most cases of English merchants and manufacturers
to buy patents of nobility after 1688[11] – is here forestalled by
the passing of the estate to the industrialist's working-class
nephew. It is he who is left to bring industry to Wanley.

Mr Wyvern, the vicar, refers to it regretfully as the passing
of Pan and quotes from Socrates' prayer in the *Phaedrus*. The
mythical animistic conception of nature's indwelling spirit which
he invokes would seem to correspond in certain respects to
Comte's conception of the 'theological' or 'fictitious' phase of
knowledge. Yet Wyvern has been a socialist in his youth and
stands for a predominantly liberal, circumspect, secularised view
of the Church's role. He renounces the appeal to dogma or
superstition. Though he shares Wyvern's regret for the passing of
the old order, Hubert Eldon has also passed beyond the intellectual
securities of the 'theological' phase. Gazing on the 'benighted
valley', he recollects a time of boyhood innocence and security:

> Was it even then nineteenth century? Not for him, seeing that
> the life of each of us reproduces the successive ages of the
> world. Belwick, roaring a few miles away, was but an isolated
> black patch on the earth's beauty, not, as he now understood
> it, a malignant cancer-spot, spreading day by day. (VII, 78)

Here it is the Comtist 'law' of recapitulation, as much as
the actual death of the old order, which marks the origin of
Eldon's sense of mutability and political disillusionment. He is
not finally a representative of the old order, but an 'insurgent'
for whom 'the detritus of convention and class prejudice' has
been thinned by 'nineteenth-century influences' (XIII). His 'fall',
like the Shakespearean 'cease of majesty', engages a social as
well as a personal dimension. Initially it is seen through the

eyes of the community as a fall from purity; but later it is identified by the narrator as an 'emancipation' which marks the beginning of 'intellectual manhood'. Adela is in some respects the valley's last innocent. Her intellectual journey takes her from theological certitude to a final transcendence of the welter of competing egotisms. The determining element of this spiritual victory is not in the final phase a Comtist historigraphy, but the idea of 'culture' as the higher synthesis of the parallel histori-ography of Hebraism and Hellenism found in Arnold's writings.

Initially Adela represents the fundamental Puritanism or Hebraism of nineteenth-century English life as it manifests itself in the cloistered existence of middle-class, 'white-souled' maidenhood. Her conflict of emotional impulse and moral duty is resolved by a narrow and disastrous adherence to the latter in an age when it has ceased to have any absolute status. The language of Puritan prayer and servitude shapes her doom:

> Adela could not bring herself to believe that 'to love' in the sense of the marriage service and 'to be in love' as her heart understood it were one and the same thing. The Puritan of her training led her to distrust profoundly those impulses of mere nature. (XII, 156)

The point here is that Adela's refusal of Eldon is really a refusal of that aesthetic and emotional side of her nature which alone might temper the rigidity of her 'Puritan maidenhood'. In choosing Mutimer Adela unconsciously embraces the dominant philosophical materialism of the nineteenth century.

The 'New Wanley Scheme' itself is offered as a satirical exposure of the egoism that directs democratic fervour, and the moral and aesthetic poverty of working-class aims. The terms of the thesis are specifically Arnoldian. Mutimer's deficiencies are indicated by the absence of English literature from his shelves; his hard-hearted egoism in personal and public life is located in this 'fatal defect'. His desertion of his working-class sweetheart, Emma Vine, to marry Adela is used to discredit his democratic zeal: 'A suggestion that domestic perfidy was in the end incompatible with public zeal would have seemed to him ridiculous, and for the simple reason that he recognised no moral sanctions' (X). His later heartless dismissal of one of his workmen demonstrates a growing despotism and paranoia (XX). The incident is placed alongside the question of Adela's instruction of the children of their new industrial community. Mutimer displays a crass utilitarian scorn for fairy-tales that is reminiscent of Gradgrind's reverence for facts over fancy. The novel's critique, in other words, is directed against the cultural deficiencies of nineteenth-century materialism, from which socialism is seen to emanate.

Yet when we come to examine the actual configuration of this negative account of 'democratic capitalism', we encounter a curious contradiction that has always discomforted critics of *Demos*. For what this critique amounts to in reality is a rejection of capitalism in its liberal humanist phase. Mutimer, as critics have recognised, is really a surrogate capitalist, and the New Wanley Scheme a fictional analogue of the type of Owenite co-operation of New Lanark long discredited among socialists as simply an attempt to moralise capitalism along paternalistic, authoritarian lines without altering the basic system of economic privilege and appropriation of surplus value.[12] Moreover in moving to Wanley, Mutimer and his mother are alienated from their true selves, their relationships increasingly mediated by messages and go-betweens. It is one of the novel's paradoxes that what is clearly meant to support its thesis that working people given instant wealth will be corrupted, should so nearly become a criticism of the alienated life-style of the owner of capital, and a recognition of the real human contact and community enjoyed by the urban poor. Mutimer does not claim to dispense with his capitalist legacy: 'Capitalists? Was he not one himself? Aye, but he would prove himself such a one as you do not meet with every day . . . he would be the glorified representative of his class' (V). The significance of his failure lies in the end not in questions of whether Gissing has prefigured the inevitable course of socialism in authoritarianism and executive power – this may or may not be true – it lies in the novel's subversion of those very liberal humanist solutions which alone appear to provide the basis of its own cultural critique and potential fictional resolution.

On an ideological level, *Demos* unconsciously exposes the illusory opposition between Gissing's attachment to culture and the implicitly positivistic historiography against which it represents a reaction. The explanation here is necessarily theoretical. For in so far as they both offer themselves as blueprints of social change, both constitute, in the final analysis, conservative reformist solutions to the problem of liberalism in post-Enlightenment industrial society with its directing ideal of the free individual. In this respect Comte's positivism is no less an idealism than Arnold's ideal of culture in its appeal to ideas as the dynamic of history and social change, and in its centring of the ethical in the transcendent individual. There are of course ideological differences. The idealists such as Arnold sought to preserve Christian values in the new secular society, whereas positivists like Frederic Harrison aspired to a scientifically based culture free of idealism. Yet Comte's own recognition of the possibility of a return to religious myth for its poetry and spiritual edification bears more than a superficial resemblance to Arnold's literary evangelism with its pervasive belief that 'the strongest part of our religion today is its unconscious poetry'.[13] Indeed the basic conservatism of Comte's philosophy results in that 'religion of humanity' whose fundamental idealism is exposed in Gissing's first novel in the figure of Helen Norman. The Comtist doctrine and the Arnoldian ideal are in a sense identical twins in terms of their conservative social morality, doomed to battle eternally in the illusory realms of ideology. Here in *Demos*, however, Gissing's depiction of the social conflicts of the 1880s in terms of these ideological differences becomes the basis of a factitious and wholly illusory transcendence.

The frailty of Gissing's idealism is evident if we compare his 'story of English socialism' with the sustained polemic against nineteenth-century Utopian theories in *The Devils*. The rejection of Utopianism depends in both works on the identification of all forms of radicalism with atheism, and the correlation of socialism, particularly in its later phase, with nineteenth-century positivism and scientism. The first frame of reference produces in both works an image of warring and finally destructive egoisms. There are some interesting parallels, for instance, between the schism in *Demos* and the conflict between the idealistic fathers and the nihilistic sons in *The Devils*, correspondences which may derive in both instances from a reworking of the generational theme in *Barnaby Rudge*. The second frame of reference, however, indicates the altogether different and fundamentally English nature of Gissing's 'story of English socialism'. For Dostoevsky the refusal of positivism as a theoretical model supporting the ideal of a secular scientific society remains a moral refusal of nineteenth-century rationalism in both its idealistic and materialistic forms. The negative polemic is directed by an authoritarian, Christian conservative hope that paradoxically recognises the social and psychological necessity of the rationalistic idea being taken to its limit. Gissing, by contrast, challenges positivism and philosophical materialism from an anti-scientific ideal of culture whose very insufficiency is shown by the terms of his own fictive representations.

In the earlier industrial novel, for example, the threat of Chartism and labour insurgency is formally negotiated by a restoration of moral order that identifies a classless, human reality beneath the regrettable contingencies of class stratification. The terms of this resolution remain Christian and humanist. The conversion and recantation that close *Alton Locke* is only a particularly flagrant example of a formal and thematic trend. In *Demos*, however, there is no attempt to gloss the reality of class antagonism or the material basis of class difference. Arthur Waltham speaks cynically of the need for the aristocracy to pursue money in a democratic age:

> 'Our aristocrats begin to see that they can't get on without money nowadays; they can't live on family records, and they find that people won't toady to them in the old way on account of their name.' (I, 13)

The restoration of Wanley Manor to Eldon at the close of the novel does not in fact mark the restoration of a natural moral order, as, say, the union of Marney and Mowbray in Disraeli's *Sybil*. Nor does it indicate a hope for the renewal of a feudal order such as we find in Mallock.[14] Rather, it makes provision for an aesthetic withdrawal from the class conflict at the novel's core. In this way Gissing provides a fictional resolution of the contradiction between his idealistic faith in culture and a recognition of its material dependence, and more specifically between an identification of culture with the hereditary instincts of aristocracy and the desire to assert the moral centrality of the Arnoldian inner self.

The whole point of the 'reversal of fortune' motif which gives Wanley to the working-class Mutimer and in the end restores it to the aristocratic Eldon is to expose the deficiency of working-class instincts as a mark of a permanent difference of caste. As a perceptive American reviewer of the novel was to note:

> *Demos* teaches the immutability of class distinctions, and, consequently, the futility of the socialist, nay, of the democratic

movement. It is not the lack of knowledge, of education, that wrecks the Mutimers. It is the want of that subtle, indefinable superiority of character which is assumed to be incapable of attainment through generations of higher culture.[15]

The reversal of fortune also demonstrates in contradictory fashion the triumph of Adela's inner self over external circumstance. The strategy depends in large part on the exemption of the bourgeoisie from the philistinism and materialism against which the novel directs its moral. The middle-class representatives in the novel may be duped like Adela or misled in youth like Mr Wyvern into sympathy with radicalism, but they remain in intellectual terms curiously provincial and traditional figures, sympathetic to and supportive of the old aristocratic order. The socialism of Westlake, the novel's Morris-like figure, is seen finally to depend on a sense of misplaced conscience, breeding an exalted but illusory vision of the 'toiling multitudes'. Arthur Waltham's radicalism is dismissed with equal indulgence as merely the spirited phase of youthful rebellion.

The discovery of the lost will and the annulment of Mutimer's inheritance mark the beginning of Adela's emancipation from the spiritual aridity and egoism that are seen to underlie Utopian and humanitarian schemes. When Mutimer is finally killed like his Chartist great-uncle by the rioting demos he has tried to lead – the novel points its gruesome moral – the way is clear for Eldon to reclaim Adela, now strengthened but uncorrupted by circumstance. The marriage which the novel's self-fulfilling structure has carefully prepared, produces an ideally conceived fusion of culture and refinement, of bourgeois morality and aristocratic privilege, in which there is not only a restoration of the old order, but its spiritual rejuvenation. The pattern of resolution would seem in some respects to repeat the romantic closure of *The Unclassed* and *A Life's Morning*. Yet the problem of *Demos* is not so much that it returns to those liberal humanist solutions which Gissing's combative project has shown to be inadequate; but that the fear of the demos is exorcised by the restoration of a pre-industrial, essentially aesthetic retreat which would seem aimed at simply ignoring democratic unrest, rather than accommodating it in terms of the humanitarian atonements that close, for instance, *The Unclassed*.

It is the novel's lack of genuine moral positives which disturbed contemporary reviewers. The reviewer of the London *Guardian*

perhaps pin-pointed most clearly the ambiguity of the novel's conclusion. 'We are not strictly sure', he wrote, 'that a fourth volume
might not in strict consistency show Adela travelling also to the
goal of egoism – her route being the fairer but no less fatal route
of aestheticism.'[16] The restoration of the valley is not after all the
restoration of a pre-existent moral order, but rather a turning back
of history that constitutes a regression to an ineffectual state. The
image of the garden retreat that closes the novel is closer in some
respects to H. G. Wells's apocalyptic world of *The Time Machine*,
with its effete Eloi threatened by the predatory Morlocks, than,
say, to Mallock's refurbished feudalism. It is this which makes
Wyvern's Carlylean appeal for an end to the cash-nexus not only
feeble, but simply irrelevant. Having already demonstrated that
the moral centrality of the old order has passed, and that the
possibility of moralising capitalism by altruism or by radicalism
is illusory, all that is left the novel is a self-fulfilling dream of
release in which inner culture is supported by the material props
of wealth and privilege. If literary aestheticism can no longer be
offered as the moral basis of a liberal humanist solution to personal
and social crisis, it remains for Gissing a critical category, a mode
of personal resistance and retreat from an inauthentic world. If in
his novels of the 1880s, Gissing ultimately refuses the possibility
of an inner self safe from the 'world's tumult', here, in the figure
of Adela, his desire is granted an imaginary transcendence.

III   THE PERMANENCE OF DIFFERENCE: *THYRZA*

'I am living at present in Lambeth', Gissing wrote to his sister
Margaret in July 1886, 'doing my best to get at the meaning
of that strange world, so remote from our civilisation.'[17] *Thyrza*
(1887) marks a significant shift in Gissing's treatment of the
condition of the people and in his perception of social conflict.
The predominantly satirical view of working-class aims and
capacities that we find in *Demos* gives way in *Thyrza* to a more
richly perceptive and authentic representation of the diversity
of working-class life and character.

In *Thyrza* as in *Demos* there is a refashioning of the melodramatic
love-story derived from the earlier industrial novel. The love-affair
between Egremont and Thyrza recalls the love-affair between the
aristocrat Charles Egremont and the 'Daughter of the People' in

Disraeli's *Sybil*; yet here the affair does not lead to a symbolic resolution of social and cultural crisis in marriage, but to an image of unbridgeable distance and permanent difference between the classes. *Thyrza* also differs significantly from *Demos* in that the emergence of materialism and industrialism is no longer attributed to working people, nor identified with Utopian ideals in order to sink them all together. Instead it is linked with economic forces, and specifically with a gross utilitarianism which is seen to augur the complete cultural and moral collapse of society. The real enemy of Egremont, the idealistic reformer, is not the working man, but the political careerist, Dalmaine. It is with this 'incarnate ideal of British philistinism' that Egremont must do battle for the soul of the people.

Egremont's plan for bringing liberal education to the upper artisans and mechanic class in Lambeth has as its historical context the whole process of middle-class intervention in the 1880s. The intensification of collectivist action and social debate in this period was in large part the result of middle-class fears. After 1850 and the defeat of Chartism, these tended to centre on the slum enclaves of London with its segregated poor. More specifically it resulted from the failure of earlier educational remedies to silence the voice of democratic protest. Egremont's programme of literary education opposes the bland utilitarianism and economic nationalism of educational control; it also seeks to counteract the dangers of propagandists making commercial and political capital out of the semi-literacy of the working classes.

In characterising his educational programme, Egremont invokes Ruskin's *Sesame and Lilies*. Ruskin's emphasis on the need to provide the material requisites that support art and civilised life is clearly echoed in Egremont's limitation of his scheme to the upper artisan who is 'not likely to fall into privation'; but the actual terms of his 'freemasonry' of cultured disciples, purifying the 'mud at the bottom of society', are also unmistakably Arnoldian. His faith in literary education as a means of morally strengthening the people against the external nature of industrial civilisation reiterates the fundamental tenets of Arnold's conception of culture as 'an inward condition of mind and spirit . . . at variance with the mechanical and material civilization'.[18] Egremont's fear of the potentially corrosive influence of scientific education on man's aesthetic and ethical heritage – a fear projected in the novel in the resistance of Jo Bunce and

Luke Ackroyd – corresponds moreover to Arnold's humanistic challenge to Huxley and the scientists in the curriculum debate. There is a third element in Egremont's liberal plan for social amelioration which identifies it as Arnoldian. This lies in his shift from literature to the 'apostolicism' of his 'Thoughts for the Present', in which he appeals in aesthetic terms to Christianity purified of dogma, and poetry charged with ethical content. Egremont, as the workmen who attend his lectures realise, is 'preaching a religion'. His programme is explicitly evangelical: 'it is the religious spirit that we must seek to revive', he tells his audience. 'Dogma will no longer help us. Pure love of moral and intellectual beauty must take its place' (VIII).

The actual germ of Egremont's idea of spiritual education is sown by the story of the little girl of ten who is sent anti-Christian comic papers by her father while she is staying at the 'Home' of the social benefactress, Mrs Ormonde (II). It is characteristic of Gissing's greater playfulness and irony in this novel that the child should later appear as Bessie Bunce, whose locksmith father attends Egremont's lectures. The actual resilience and psychological complexity of family life in the Bunce household, which we glimpse in a series of distanced yet wry vignettes, rebounds in an ironic way on Egremont's middle-class condescension, and on his mechanistic view of human learning and capacities. This is an important recognition. One of the most vital aspects of the novel is its appreciative view of the positive aspects of working class life – of its musical traditions, its 'friendly lead', and of the resilience and friendships of the factory girl, Totty Nancarrow, one of Gissing's most original creations. It is a recognition of an alternative culture to Egremont's 'sweetness and light'. In *Thyrza* the account of working-class culture is neither patronisingly sentimental, as in, say, Maugham and Morrison, nor suggestive, as in James's *The Princess Casamassima*, of an aesthetic fascination with the uncharted haunts of a 'semi-human' London poor.

For someone like Bunce, who has fallen from his position of successful locksmith to unemployed journeyman, the sacrifice and submission that Egremont's aestheticised Christianity demands might have been possible in a hierarchical society in which worth is finally divorced from social status. In a stratified secular society, such a submission becomes an act of self-humiliation, an admission of failure which must be refused. To Luke Ackroyd, the politicised workman, Egremont's religion of culture is merely 'Sops to the dog that's beginning to show his teeth! . . . It shows you what's coming. The capitalists are beginning to look about and ask what they can do to keep the people quiet' (III). Culture in Ackroyd's eyes is simply another palliative to working-class unrest. Its purpose is not to liberate working people, but to 'keep them quiet'. Egremont's 'Thoughts for the Present' are, by his own admission, intended 'to persuade them to forget that there are such things as questions of the day' (XI). As Egremont is the son of an oil-cloth manufacturer in Lambeth, and thus a beneficiary of capitalism, the ambiguity of his offer of aesthetic consolation would seem to stand fully exposed.

Yet this recognition of the resistance of the people to culture from above throws into partial relief the covert strategy not only of the hero's liberal humanist prescriptions, but also of the narrator's own resolutely distancing view of working-class life. In one of the most revealing passages in *Thyrza*, the novel's sensitive and literate workman, Gilbert Grail, pauses in his solitary walk through Lambeth on Christmas Eve to listen to the street organ. In its 'vulgar clanging of melody', the narrator tells us, 'the secret of hidden London' is 'half-revealed'. The focus is upon Grail's mute response, on his watchful oneness with those who live in 'the unmapped haunts of the semi-human'. But the experience of pathos is generalised; it is the narrator who speaks. The secret of hidden London lies in

> The life of men who toil without hope, yet with the hunger of an unshaped desire . . . the careless defiance of the youth who feels his blood and revolts against the lot which would tame it; all that is purely human in these darkened multitudes speaks to you as you listen. It is the half conscious striving of a nature which knows not what it would attain, which deforms a true thought by gross expression, which clutches at the beautiful and soils it with foul hands.   (IX, 111–12)

It is true, as Adrian Poole has argued,[19] that this passage goes to the heart of a recurrent contradiction in Gissing's early 'social novels' – an emotional friction between revulsion from the 'gross expression' of the 'semi-human', and an imaginative identification with 'all that is purely human' in the 'darkened multitudes'. And yet the actual force of that recognition of vitality and aspiration by the lonely watcher, who feels 'the difference and distance' yet who identifies with the desire and revolt, is not simply passive. Underlying it is a palpable fear and need to incorporate those whose *carpe diem* challenges the conditions under which they live, and whose blood revolts against 'the lot which would tame it'.

The authorial position is shot through in effect with the same ambiguity which underlies the hero's programme of reform, with its liberal humanist appeal to a common humanity. It is this correspondence which accounts for the seemingly wilful blindness and evasions in the novel's account of his failure. Specifically, the novel's ironic rejection of Egremont's literary evangelism rests in the end on an overarching determinism and static conception of class which strategically suppresses the evident ambiguity of his motives. We see here the basis of Gissing's own fictional solution to the central conflict in the industrial novel between conscience and middle-class fear of democracy. In *Thyrza* that resolution can no longer be achieved by the plot – Gissing's novels after all deliberately subvert the inherited Romantic motifs of the genre. Rather, Gissing's solution lies in a fatalistic suspension of the historical process itself. In this way his 'idiom of observation, of a generalised and distancing compassion'[20] can combine with a refusal of the total social order in which the lower classes are nevertheless kept securely in their place.

Egremont's cultural crusade is seen to fail because it is ultimately irrelevant to people who have their own forms of cultural consolation and release. Higher culture may even have a debilitating effect on the working man since it feeds longings that cannot be realised, and ultimately magnifies his alienation from his world. If in *Demos* the absence of English literature from Mutimer's library is used to measure the spiritual deficiency of working-class instincts, their presence in Grail's bookcase indicates the inevitable estrangement of the cultured workman from his life of necessary toil. As he goes out in the early morning to the candle and soap factory where he works, the 'wondrous promises' of his nightly reading turn to a death-wish 'to lie down and lose consciousness of the burden of life' (IX). Even when the 'golden prospect' of a more integrated life becomes possible with Egremont's offer of a librarian's post in Lambeth, it serves to focus more clearly his inescapable homelessness. On visiting the school where the library is to be housed, he feels a 'distressing dejection creep upon him' (IX). A recognition of the limits of that prospect of emotional and intellectual freedom is made more explicit as he walks abroad in search of an external correlative for his inner joy; for his journey of celebration is confined to streets whose sounds and odours are familiar. The 'obscure magnitude' of the Houses of Parliament and the 'low-grey shape' of Westminster Abbey – monumental emblems of political power and cultural tradition on the other side of Lambeth Bridge – remain remote and unattainable. Unlike Hardy's Jude, who battles with the obstructive circumstances of a refusing society, Grail – and the novel itself – accepts those barriers as absolute.

An appeal to existing social arrangements also extenuates Egremont's desertion of Thyrza, a work-girl whose social and artistic refinement, as one early reviewer astutely observed, 'is perhaps accounted for by the fact that her mother was a teacher'[21]. Thyrza is engaged to be married to Grail, but is drawn irresistibly to Egremont whose stories of life beyond Lambeth make 'her inward sight an awful reality'. Yet for Thyrza too the bridge is the symbolic barrier to the realisation of her desire for an existence 'beyond and above the life which was her lot'. It is there at their final meeting that Egremont deserts her before they have reached the Westminster side of the river and 'his own part of the town' (XXII). Though Thyrza may pose a challenge to the 'naturalised' barriers of class and privilege – her singing voice can charm Mrs Ormonde's drawing room as well as move the workers at the 'friendly lead' – she is destined to remain in Lambeth. The desertion itself comes to be seen as a recognition of real class barriers. It is this which lies behind Mrs Ormonde's 'prudential forecasts and schemings' to keep them apart and finally daunts Egremont's belated plan to marry Thyrza later in the novel:

He knew what miseries had again and again resulted from marriages such as this, and he feared for her quite as much as for himself. For there was no more passion. (XXXVII, 444)

Egremont is finally allowed to renounce his former idealism as a mere 'dilettantism' because it failed to take account of the realities of life.

The novel, however, also admits another reason for Egremont's desertion that is much more problematic. In Mrs Ormonde's view it is not Thyrza but Egremont who is 'found wanting'. It is clear that her accusation is directed against Egremont's conventionality. 'You have little real energy', she tells him. 'You are passive in great trials; it is easier for you to suffer than to act. Your idealism is often noble, but never heroic' (XXVIII). She considers him unworthy of Thyrza and stands in shame of her own actions:

> Egremont's perishable love, her own prudential forecasts and schemings, were stamped poor, worldly, ignoble, in comparison with this sacred and extinguishable ardour.   (XXXVIII, 455)

'Extinguishable' here has a curious force, with its suggestion not of inevitability, but of calculation. It directs us not to the inadequacy of passivity and conventionality, but the active duplicity involved in keeping the existing social order intact.

The efforts to exclude Thyrza reveal not so much the limitation of Egremont's love for the people, but its ambiguity. Paradoxically it is this dark underside of motive which his desertion has attempted to keep hidden. For to bear Thyrza to 'his own part of the town' would be to make visible his desire to appropriate that 'passionate instinct' he detects in the 'darkened multitudes'. What we are faced with is the unforeseen consequence of Gissing's subversion of the conventional structure of sentiment and melodrama. In refusing to flatter the spectacle of middle-class philanthropy or to invoke the consolatory convention of hypergamy, the narrative lays bare not only the inherent idealism of these fictional motifs, but the ideological strategies that underpin them. Thyrza is inextricably bound up with Grail's 'golden prospect'; in order to win her, Egremont must of necessity rob his protégé of the one being who brings a sense of joy and independence to his subordinate and sacrificial life. Similarly Thyrza's choice of Egremont may satisfy her desire for social elevation, but it also necessitates her betrayal of Grail and Lambeth. Hers is the intolerable dilemma of Emily Hood in *A Life's Morning*, torn between cultural aspiration and the loyalties of home. The novel threatens in effect to reveal the class conflicts underlying its central motivation, and thus rob itself of its own idealistic centre and means of resolution.

The novel's conclusion is finally predictable. The threat of revolt is dispelled in an image of frustrated aspiration. There is a general acceptance of the actual over the ideal in the segregated worlds of the classes. Prescription and protest yield to personal preoccupations. Bunce marries Totty Nancarrow;

Thyrza returns to Lambeth to die; and Grail reconciles himself to his lot. Even the hot-headed Ackroyd ceases to 'trouble himself about politics, and religion, and social matters' which Egremont's idealism is seen paradoxically to have provoked in him. Instead he returns to his former study of chemistry. In the final scenes the working people are all in their place, and Egremont himself returns to the country house and a defeated idealism.

And yet the resolution of the novel's tensions in a static conception of class is not simply a fictional illusion; it involves a rationalisation of existing social arrangements which corresponds to an available mode of cognition. In *Thyrza* this becomes the basis for an assertion of inner selfhood and a cultured elite in a materialistic age. Egremont's encomium to Thyrza's 'gift of passionate imagination' as he examines the chalk portrait by the unknown artist is made to serve a conveniently fatalistic view of life. Thyrza's ideal is characterised with comforting pathos as unearthly. Her inner life, like Grail's cultural aspiration and Egremont's own idealism, is seen finally to bow to the overriding forces of circumstance. The novel may demonstrate the triumph of philistinism and 'practical philanthropy' in the figure of Dalmaine, but Egremont's idealism is granted moral centrality. At the end of the novel Egremont celebrates the spiritual in man in his discovery of Whitman. Through Whitman, he writes, 'the healthy unconscious man, the "average man", utters what before he had no voice to tell of, the secret aspirations, his mute love and praise' (XXXV). There is a return here to the affirmations of the 'street organ' passage. Indeed for Gissing himself, who confessed to weeping while he wrote the final chapters of the novel, Thyrza was 'one of the most beautiful dreams I ever had or shall have'.[22] The whole force of the novel, however, would seem to question such sentimentality. For Thyrza is no mute voice; she speaks of a desire for social elevation which exposes the insufficiency and ambiguity of Egremont's cultural crusade. It is a desire which not only slips through the suppressions and evasions of the novel's own enforced harmonisation and rationalisation of existing conditions, but rebounds with continuing significance on history itself. For it is one of the novel's enduring ironies that the ideal of 'missionaries of culture', and of the unifying tendency of literary education through its appeal to common language and culture, should become the basis of the Newbolt Report (1921) over thirty years later, and an influential ideology of education even as I write.

IV VICTIMS OF CIRCUMSTANCE: *THE NETHER WORLD*

The Nether World (1889) is unquestionably the most successful and compelling of Gissing's novels on 'the condition of the people'. The novel clearly bears the mark of that resurgence of social indignation and Hogarthian purpose which Gissing experienced on learning of the sordid and miserable death of his estranged first wife, Nell Harrison:

> I did my utmost; again and again I had her back to me. Fate was too strong. But as I stood beside that bed, I felt that my life henceforth had a finer purpose. Henceforth I would never cease to bear testimony against the accursed social order that brings about things of this kind.[23]

The brutal accuracy of his account of working-class life in Clerkenwell introduced a new kind of realism to the English public. As generations of readers have discovered, there is quite simply no novel like it in English fiction.

It must be said that the novel's energy depends to some extent on those exaggerated representations of working-class life and character which have always been the stock-in-trade of English writers, linking Dickens's underworld with the working-class England of Arthur Morrison, Somerset Maugham and the Graham Greene of *Brighton Rock*. In *The Nether World* we have the 'booze and violence' of the Crystal Palace outing, with its images of excess and criminality, as well as the sensational set pieces of popular melodrama in the vitriol attack on the stage-struck Clara Hewett, and the hunting down of her brother Bob for counterfeiting. Yet the real force of the novel clearly lies elsewhere, in the humanising perspective through which these images of working-class energy are made to appear pathetically, even representatively human. The novel, for instance, is completely free of the sentimentalising strain which we find in the 'industrial novel' of the 1840s and 1850s, and indeed to some extent in Gissing's own earlier novels on the condition of the people. Absent too is any representative middle-class character through whom the novel might hold out a consolatory vision of refuge or retreat. The plot itself involves a wholesale subversion of the philanthropic romance: the wealth of Michael Snowdon, the rich and venerable philanthropist who has returned from Australia, is preyed upon by avaricious predators in a world dominated by self-interest. Even Jane Snowdon, the Dickensian figure of innate goodness whom old Snowdon makes the reluctant bearer of his own egotistical dreams, is shown in the end to be spiritless and wholly ineffectual in a world whose only law is the 'survival of the fittest'. Gissing here seems at last to achieve the goal he set himself at the beginning of the 1880s of writing a novel totally antithetical to anything in Dickens. Indeed it is the relentlessness with which the novel questions the remedies of Christians and social reformers to the problem of the London poor which finally appeared hateful to many contemporary readers, even those like Dean Farrer who recognised that Gissing's novel was 'disastrously true'.[24]

Admittedly there is something consolatory even in this bleakest and most pessimistic of social visions. It is not only that the novel's imagery and narrative paradigms of entrapment serve what Frederic Jameson has characterised as a 'mystification and legitimation' of existing social arrangements.[25] That consolation also lies to some extent in the self-exemptions of the narrative voice itself with its strains of moralism and contempt for 'the people'.

There is evidently a connection between Gissing's vision of physical and spiritual entrapment in *The Nether World* and the urban landscapes of later twentieth-century novelists and poets of the urban revolution; but the tone and effect of Gissing's novel would seem to link his London more closely to the place of 'chaos and dread night' of Pope's *Dunciad* than, say, to Eliot's 'unreal city' or Joyce's synoptic Dublin. The classical references; the generalisation of working-class faults; the self-dramatising asides: these tend to suggest an attitude of difference and condescension shared by both narrator and reader towards the novel's working-class characters. There is nothing in the actual narration of the collective voice of the city or the people; nothing, say, of the *style indirect libre* of *L'Assommoir*, which was an attempt by Zola to avoid the more obvious prejudices and attitudes presented in the language of his own class. The use of classical references in *The Nether World*, particularly in the 'Io Saturnalia' sequence which describes the Bank Holiday outing to the Crystal Palace, not only indicates that Gissing is 'not writing for working people';[26] it also measures a distance and enforces a standard. The voice of cultural protest in this case may be fundamentally irrational and defeatist, given the novel's Social Darwinian vision of absolute struggle as the law of life; but more than this, it becomes a means of evading the duplicity and ambiguity of its own contradictory moralism and self-exemption.

Consider, for instance, the scene at the beginning of the novel in which the working-class hero, Sidney Kirkwood, pleads with the wayward Clara to return to her family. After recording Clara's angry refusal, the narrator suddenly betrays the observed nature of much of his account of working-class life:

> How often, in passing along the streets, one catches a few phrases of discord such as this! The poor can seldom command privacy; their scenes alike of tenderness and of anger must for the most part be enacted on the peopled ways. It is one of their misfortunes, one of the many necessities which blunt feeling, which balk reconciliation, which enhance the risks of dialogue at best semi-articulate. (X, 93)

There is a movement here characteristic of *The Nether World* – the observation of the distanced narrator, the sympathetic recognition of the force of circumstance and, finally, the instinctive prejudice which undercuts the voice of protest and initial sympathy. The roots of this prejudice (that the dialogue of the poor is at best semi-articulate) lies in a confusion of difference with deficiency. This is the basis of some of the novel's most outrageous asides – the view, for instance, that 'irony is not a weapon much in use among working people; their wits in general are too slow'; or the assertion that the London poor are the 'least original and least articulate beings within the confines of civilisation' on the grounds that among them an indignant tone 'reserved for an expression of offence among educated people . . . has to do the duty for friendly emphasis'.

Kirkwood himself is in many respects a characteristic Gissing hero. Like Gissing's other unclassed intellectual heroes, he has undergone a change of heart from social conscience to self-cultivation. The ironic, almost disdainful rhetoric of the novel itself would seem to support his refusal of both the radical-ism of Clara's father, John Hewett, and the supreme egotism and futility of Snowdon's philanthropic ideal. By marrying the disfigured and defeated Clara, Kirkwood is seen to turn man's fundamental 'will to live' against itself in a Schopenhauerian act of pity and renunciation. Yet there is something uncomfortable about the final approving images of Kirkwood's triumphant sacrifice which would seem to identify it with those middle-class appeals for thrift and sobriety scornfully rejected by Michael Snowdon: 'poor people are expected to practice a self-denial that the rich can't even imagine, much less carry out!'(XX). Kirkwood, we might argue, stands in the final analysis not as a culture hero, but as a middle-class version of the exemplary working man – obedient, sober, industrious and self-denying.

All this may be commonplace. Yet I think it is wrong to devalue the novel for portraying a fatalistic universe and a static conception of existing conditions. For what the novel forces us to recognise is that fatalism itself is a habit of mind and defensive gesture engendered by wounded self-esteem. The real significance of *The Nether World* lies then in the revelation of the defensive, sometimes self-lacerating strategies of autonomy and identity which are the historical reality and lived experience of lower-class life in a stratified and refusing social order. The lust of Mrs Peckover and her daughter Clem for 'sanguinary domination' may be attributed to the inherent savagery of human nature beneath the veneer of civilisation, but there is a suggestion too that it represents 'a strong sense of personal dignity' driven to adopt the acquisitive and brutal forces of an inhuman system. The roots of defiance and irrational self-will are located throughout the novel in frustrated energy and a thwarted sense of personal worth.

This is vividly and painfully rendered in the progress of the Hewett family. Old John Hewett with his dyed hair and his dwindling parental authority is a victim not only of circumstance, but of his own stubborn pride and self-will. In him the forces of oppression are 'ludicrously personified'. His daughter Clara displays an equally debilitating internalisation of social pressures. Scawthorne, the shadowy sexual predator, is to her 'a mere abstraction, the representative of a wild hope'. Through her contractual promiscuity, she accepts the terms of a depersonalising, inhuman system. The message is pressed home with explicit force:

> Natures such as hers are as little to be judged by that which is conventionally the highest standard as by that which is the lowest. The tendencies which we agree to call good and bad became in her merely directions of a native force which was at all times in revolt against circumstance. Characters thus moulded may go far in achievement. . . . As often as our conventions give us the opportunity, we crush them out of being;

they are noxious; they threaten the frame of society. Oftenest the crushing is done in such a way that the hapless creatures seem to have brought about their own destruction.   (XXXII, 295)

It is not Clara who is at fault but the social system which *moulds* her and sets the traps with which she will destroy herself. Bondage in the nether world is not simply external but psychological.

This is demonstrated most clearly in Clara's return to Kirkwood after her disfigurement in the vitriol attack, which ends her dream of becoming an actress. Here we see that her subsequent survival with dignity depends on a subservience to Kirkwood's own defensive self-sacrifice. Her final choice of self-humiliation in the face of the humiliating refusals of the social order is directed significantly by the same pathological impulse that characterised her original resistance to her father's domination. The novel perceptively pin-points the social and psychological currents of defiance and self-ruin:

The access of self-pity was followed, as always, by a persistent sense of intolerable wrong, and that again by a fierce desire to plunge herself into ruin, as though by such an act she could satiate her instincts of defiance.   (X, 94)

Her desire to regain Kirkwood's love is motivated by a self-pitying rebellion against 'the martyrdom' she has suffered; again, however, it plunges her into a sado-masochistic relationship. She chooses to humiliate herself in order to 'command homage' and 'make for herself a dominion' (XXXII). Clara and Kirkwood are both victims, each bound to the psychology of sacrifice.

It is on this note that the novel ends. The house at Crouch End where 'poverty hides itself with venetian blinds' mocks the hope that the problems of overcrowding and misery can be resolved by model dwellings. Not only does the standard of housing actually fall – the 'whole fabric' is 'a thing of lath and sand' – but it lacks the human contact of the old rookeries. In the final, horrifying descriptions of life at Crouch End, the pattern of entrapment and self-ruin become absolute. Even the Hewett children are bound inexorably to the psychology of sacrifice and betrayal:

Of every mouthful that they ate, the price was known to them. The roof over their heads was there by no grace of Providence, but solely because such-and-such a sum was paid weekly in hard cash, when the collector came.   (XXXIX, 368–9)

Kirkwood's is a sacrifice that demands submission and sacrifice in return. He blames his personal failure on adverse circumstances; but as his final appeal to Clara shows, his rationale of sacrifice for the sake of the children is really an attempt to make up for his own shortcomings:

> 'Look, Clara, you and I are going to do what we can for these children; we're not going to give up the work now we've begun it. Mustn't all of us who are poor stand together and help one another?'   (XXXIX, 378)

This is not a plea for defiance and solidarity, but for enslavement in a mutual sacrifice that demands subservience. Gissing offers here an almost unbearably accurate account of the real conditions of bondage among the poor for whom oppression is not simply external but internal, an amalgam of sexual and social pressure and roles that, for all the hopes of the reformers, perhaps remains the greatest obstacle to social change.

4

The Measure of Success: from *The Emancipated* to *New Grub Street*

> *The measure of his bitterness is the measure of his love of good.*
>
> Virginia Woolf

George Gissing's biographers have generally attributed his abandonment of working-class themes to the influences of his first extended visit abroad.[1] The feeling of spiritual expansion he experienced after his escape from London, as well as the conflicts he felt between his cultural tourism and the realities of the places he visited – these undoubtedly fuelled a

> dislike of everything that concerns the life of the people. Paris has even become distasteful to me because I am living in this quarter, in a house thronged with workpeople, and where, to get away, I must always pass through dirty and swarming streets. All my interest in such things I have left behind in London. On crossing the Channel, I have become a poet pure and simple, or perhaps it would be better to say an idealist student of art.[2]

Yet Gissing's decision to abandon working-class themes had already been taken before he left England. Even while writing *The Nether World* he had professed his weariness of 'all this idealism'.[3] It is a curious expression to use of a novel which focuses with

82

such savage and uncompromising realism on the compelling necessities of working-class life. It would seem to refer in fact to the mood of resurgent radicalism that directed his writing of the book, and in particular to that vow 'to bear testimony against the accursed social order' which he had taken after the death of his first wife.[4] For Gissing, the novel's idealism clearly lies in its implicit hope of improvement and social change.

In the novels that followed, Gissing continued to challenge the spiritual bankruptcy of industrial society, but his project is no longer infected with images of class conflict and fears of democratic unrest. It is significant that Gissing's first novel after *The Nether World*, *The Emancipated*, should render Arnold's ideal of culture in such clear, unproblematic outlines. It is a novel which constitutes an artful, almost self-deceiving pause between Gissing's unflinching vision of 'the condition of the people' and his thematic return to the harsh realities of urban life in *New Grub Street*.

Written immediately after his first journey to Italy, *The Emancipated* clearly reflects something of the lingering mood of spiritual uplift this experience had inspired.[5] The journey itself was not without its ambivalent side. In particular it served to quicken his sense of the inherent 'Hebraism' of English life. Both of these moods are reflected in *The Emancipated*. It is a work of some psychological insight, notably in the account of the heroine's struggles with her Puritan heritage. Yet it is a novel which has never found favour with the critics. The reason for this lies in the uncomfortably transparent way in which it reveals its message.

The Emancipated sets out to demonstrate the inadequacy of unbridled liberalism and unsweetened Hebraism in the contrasted histories of Cecily Doran and Miriam Baske. Cecily is an heiress who represents modernity and emancipation from prejudice; Miriam is a wealthy widow marked with the 'cold austerity' of English Puritanism. Through its account of the disillusionments and ultimate disintegration of Cecily's hasty marriage to Miriam's brother, Reuben, the novel registers a moral critique of the dangerous excesses and superficiality of modern liberalism. At the same time, it embodies the moral possibility of a marriage between dogma and enlightenment, Hebraism and Hellenism, in Miriam's deepening involvement with the artist, Ross Mallard. The problem of personal authenticity, here as elsewhere in Gissing's work, also engages the problem of authentic art. Cecily elevates the artist above 'the rules by which common people must direct their lives" (II). Miriam censures the life of the artist as 'frivolous, if not something worse' (V). Her marriage to Mallard at the close of the novel is clearly meant to represent a synthesis of 'sweetness and light' that balances the enslaving excesses of liberalism and the numbing effects of dogma.

It is a synthesis in which Jacob Korg has identified 'a curious symmetry of design not found in Gissing's other novels'[6]. This can be seen to lie in the novel's almost allegorical mode of representation. The novel focuses, on an interpersonal level, on the crisis that engaged Arnold in *Culture and Anarchy* – on the need for the English middle-class to 'Hellenise' itself. The search for an ideology capable of transcending a superannuated traditionalism and a dangerously progressive liberalism is here displaced, as in Arnold's polemic, to the abstract plane of ideas and immutable categories, which allow for an ethical resolution. This is effected by the novel's careful orchestration of ideological tensions and contradictions. The unresolved split in English social and intellectual life between traditionalism and liberalism is conveniently embodied, for instance, in Miriam and Reuben, as antithetical aspects of the same Puritan past. Moreover, the social injury and financial insecurity that characteristically threaten the claims of Gissing's mobile heroes to inner autonomy are here erased. Gissing is thus able to achieve a dissolution of ideological contradictions in purely ethical and personal terms, without the severe disjunctions and enforced harmonisations of his earlier novels.

The Emancipated does in fact register some disturbance to its general pattern of triumphant morality. There is a recognition, for instance, that the triumph of Miriam and Mallard is really a compromise rather than a solution, that the 'medium' they represent between Puritan conscience and liberated intellect may well be 'a neither this nor that, an insipid refinement, a taste for culture moderated by Mrs Grundy' (I). It is significant too that the characteristic traits of Gissing's earlier unclassed heroes should suddenly erupt in the scenes describing Reuben's life at Belsize Park. Reuben displays a brooding sense of social injury and failure which emerges in response to his wife's social pre-eminence; and more significantly, a struggle of almost heroic proportions between law and passion. Ultimately, however, such disturbances are banished to the margins of the work, where they lend support to the novel's Social Darwinian view of society as a place of scarcity and limited energy where each 'joy in the world' is seen to represent 'a counterbalance of sorrow' (XII).

It is this kind of concession to idealism that is ruthlessly refused in Gissing's subsequent studies of the lower middle classes. In his novels of the 1890s, philistinism is not only shown to be triumphant, but that triumph is portrayed without the suggestions of violence and gross moral disfigurement that are made to carry the note of moral censure in *The Emancipated*. *New Grub Street*, *Born in Exile*, *The Odd Women*: it is on these works that Gissing's critical reputation has come to depend. Of these, *New Grub Street* has received most praise. It is generally considered to be the summation of Gissing's achievement and the measure of his success.

New Grub Street is an insider's scandalous and embittered revelation of the inglorious truth about a writer's life and work. It is this which undoubtedly accounts for the novel's popularity among Gissing's contemporaries, and indeed with succeeding generations of readers. The squalid family quarrels, petty egotism and sexual tensions which form the human back-drop to artistic aspiration in the Yule and Reardon households; the gross practicality of the immodest, self-applauding Jasper Milvain for whom literary success depends on giving people what they want: *New Grub Street* tantalisingly lays bare the oppressive nature of literary production in a recognisably modern age of telegraphic communication and mass education. However, why such an exposure should be of significant aesthetic interest is a question which has important historical and cultural implications.

The late French structuralist, Roland Barthes, in a playful disclosure of the ideas which Western society habitually entertains about its writers, has pointed out its devotedness to presenting the mundane details of a writer's life and personality.[7] This attention, he argues, far from 'demystifying' the exaltedness of the writer, is intended to convey 'a sublime contradiction' between his 'prosaic condition' and his 'glamorous status', to make him in effect 'even more miraculous'. Barthes's irony is clearly directed against those unreflexive forms of contemporary signification such as popular journalism, but the process of mystification which he uncovers is one which can be seen systematically to shape and naturalise our conception of the creative artist in modern times. In particular, Barthes's essay directs us some way to understanding the paradoxical nature of the writer's spiritual singularity. As prey to an inner voice, the writer is a special case, someone who stands apart from other men; yet as the living embodiment of man's sense of contemporary homelessness and division, he is at the same time wholly representative. Indeed, one could argue that it is for this reason that the treatment of the writer's life is ultimately of such compelling interest. The problems of the professional writer 'in marketing his work to a larger, more urban public' are, as Marilyn Butler has argued, 'clearly related to the frustrated and alienating experience of other citizens in an increasingly complex and specialised environment'.[8] What leads novelists like Gissing to introduce writers into their work is not simply 'a natural self-absorption',[9] but a sense of the importance and centrality of their experience. The writer in effect lives out in his very labour a wider social conflict between the claims of free selfhood and the determinations of the market-place.

This is the conflict of the impotent hero of *New Grub Street*. Reardon's anguished cry that his 'imagination can shape nothing substantial' is a lament characteristic of the Romantic artist since the time of Coleridge. On one level, it represented a defensive reaction against a world inimical to art, the final symptom on occasions of a paralysis and drying-up of creative inspiration; on other occasions, however, it became the source of triumphantly successful works about the difficulty of composition itself. If the fate of Gissing's hero is a tragic instance of the former, *New Grub Street* itself is a triumphant example of the latter. What is remarkable about *New Grub Street* is its unsparing descriptions of the actual physical labour of literary composition – a fact which writers are more often compelled to suppress in compliance with common assumptions about the processes of creation. We are given unromantic accounts of Reardon's bitter struggles with the three-volume form, of Marian Yule's ink-stained labours in the British Museum, even of the single-minded application and discipline that gives the lie to Milvain's achieved facility. *New Grub Street*, as Bernard Bergonzi has pointed out, is 'the most explicit fictional study of literary life ever written in England'.[10]

In portraying the actual toil and frustrations of the professional writer, Gissing's aim is clearly to question the conditions which have reduced literature to a commodity. On one level, the novel is a counteraction to the idealisation of the creative process which nevertheless preserves the ideal of Romantic creativity intact. I will want to argue that the novel does in fact exceed such a reading, and that this interpretation results in a severe reduction of its significance and complexity; however, it must be admitted that there are good grounds for interpreting the novel in this way. Among the most important of these is the novel's evident debt and reaction to that other major fictional representation of nineteenth-century grub street – Thackeray's *Pendennis*. Gissing's response to Thackeray's novel can be traced back to 1884 and his involvement in the debate on the censureship of the circulating libraries. 'One of the most painful confessions in literature', Gissing wrote,

> is that contained in the preface of *Pendennis*, where Thackeray admits that 'since the author of *Tom Jones* was buried no writer of fiction among us has been permitted to depict to his utmost power a man,' – on penalty, be it understood, of a temporary diminution of receipts. If this be not a tradesman's attitude, what is? Let novelists be true to their artistic conscience, and the public taste will come round. In that day there will be no complaint of the circulating libraries. It is a hard thing to say, but Thackeray, when he knowingly wrote below the demands of his art to conciliate Mrs Grundy, betrayed his trust; and the same thing is being done by our living novelists every day.[11]

Gissing's praise of Thackeray's honesty becomes in effect a regretful condemnation of his 'tradesman's attitude' and conciliation of Mrs Grundy. It is clearly also a response to Thackeray's attitude to literature in the novel itself, where the youthful hero's disillusioning experience in the literary market-place becomes an occasion for healthy laughter at the idealism of youth, rather than for criticism of present degradations. Although one can find parallels and foreshadowings of *New Grub Street* in the earlier novel – notably in Warrington's practical view of the 'prose labourer', and in the descriptions of Bohemian life – there is nothing in Gissing of that cheerful acceptance of 'things as they are'. Charlotte Brontë, initially at least, considered Thackeray to be the great moralist of his age; Gissing, though he identified more fully with Thackeray than with Dickens,[12] recoiled nevertheless from Thackeray's ultimately conciliatory position. The point is not that Gissing fails to demystify Romantic notions of literary composition, rather that he goes further in that demystification in order to reaffirm ideals that have been lost sight of in an increasingly commercial age, and indeed in his predecessor's too facile acceptance of things as they are.

The interpretation of *New Grub Street* as the bitter complaint of a Romantic idealist in a grossly commercial age has proved irresistible to succeeding generations of readers. In her influential review of Gissing's work which appeared in *Scrutiny*, and in many ways typified its critical mode of responsiveness and intuition, Q. D. Leavis, for instance, isolates *New Grub Street* as Gissing's 'one permanent contribution to the English novel'.[13] In the problem of authorship, in the conflict of artistic integrity and commercial demands, Gissing, she argues, found a subject that was 'both inside him and outside him', and constituted 'his most vital interest'. It is a vital interest shared also by the critic. The tone of 'irony weighted with disgust' strikes her 'as being the right outlook' on a literary world colonised by the 'men of straw' such as Welpdale, and the mercenary publicists and journalists such as Milvain. And yet, though Mrs Leavis identifies closely with the novelist's 'vital interest', her suggestion that his disconsolate view of the literary world may be 'less suited to life in general', indicates a degree of distance and moral privilege. Compelled by her cultural attachments to accept the novel's version of cultural decline, yet constrained by the same token to refuse the absoluteness of Reardon's and Biffen's defeat, the critic is driven to seek in the novel a moral meaning that will satisfy the demands of a disinterested response, and the novel's claim to a permanent place in the literary canon:

> Delicacy and fineness, the strongly noble and the devotedly disinterested elements in human nature, are not ignored or denied, they are presented with complete success – this is the measure of Gissing's total success here – in the person of Marian Yule, whom Milvain jilts and leaves to wretchedness, and Reardon's friend Biffen who is driven to remove himself from the world that has no use for his devoted labours.[14]

The sheer evasion of this remarkable euphemism betrays the degree of repression involved in preserving the privilege of contemplative distance in reading Gissing's work.

The relationship of ideal to reality in *New Grub Street* is in fact one of absolute degradation and defeat in which there is seen to be no possibility of going outside the terms of the material world. More specifically, the novel exposes the illusory nature of Socratic freedom and autonomy in the external world of late-Victorian industrial society. The novel in this sense is a reworking of *The Unclassed*, with literary Bohemia now being refused the kind of moral authority and social transcendence granted it within the classical realist paradigms of the earlier work. This is important. For by dramatising the conflicts of Romantic humanism through its version of the career of the 'man of letters', the novel effectively exposes the inefficacy of that consolatory intellectual alienation which criticism would claim for itself. The consequence has been a certain uneasiness among critics, whose praise of *New Grub Street* is generally qualified with formal and ethical censures and reservations.

Among the most frequent of these is the expressed dissatisfaction with the novel's failure to reflect the aesthetic resistance of anti-philistine publishers and minority writers like Henry James, George Moore and indeed Gissing himself – writers who indicate the possibility of reconciling artistic integrity with public recognition.[15] Such a naïvely mimetic approach to the novel on the part of critics alerts us to the obvious fact that realism, and fiction generally, is not answerable to a total empirical reproduction of some external meaning or reality. The limitation of such a mechanistic theory of reflection is not only that it ignores the determinate nature of literary production – linguistic, genetic, cultural – not least the need to suppress 'reality' in order to say anything at all; it also erases the basis of its fictional freedom to mean more than it 'intends'.[16] The work is reduced unproblematically to the artist's subjective re-creation of the 'real world' which is seen to precede the work, and which provides criticism with its authority.

Such a view is particularly damaging in Gissing's case. It is not simply that the novel's incorrectness or inaccuracy is located condescendingly in Gissing's unhappy temperament in a way that reduces the representativeness of his position to a merely personal issue. More seriously, the reduction of the work to a single meaning – in this instance to the essentially Romantic opposition between art and trade – bypasses and suppresses its contradictions and complexities, and indeed the radical insights which spring from these, as the novel's ideological themes become the subject of aesthetic development and inscription. Specifically, the opposition of literature and trade is exceeded by a materialist split in the idea of literature itself which forbids the kind of contemplative privilege to the reader that normative procedures would seek to impose.

The basis of this creative contradiction is to be located in the first instance in the peculiarities of Gissing's own perspective. Gissing's point of view is indicated in his explanation of his title to his German correspondent, Bertz:

> In Pope and his contemporaries the name has become synonymous for wretched-authordom. In Hogarth's 'Distressed Author' there is a Grub Street somewhere inscribed. Poetry and meanness of spirit being naturally associated, the street came to denote an abode, not merely of poor, but of insignificant writers.[17]

Here then, in the image of poor and insignificant writers that he finds in the poetry of Pope and in the art of his revered Hogarth, is the basis of Gissing's thematic interest. If Gissing extends that picture of debasement to the whole literary profession, he does so not as a Romantic idealist, but from a position that looks back to the neo-classical ideal of literature. The distinction is crucial, and must be derived to some extent from the classical traditions and influences of Gissing's own liberal humanist education. For Gissing, the alternative to the contemporary subsumption of literature to trade is not in the end a Romantic ideal of an autonomous, oppositional art, but a classical and in essence social ideal of art as integral. It is this angle of vision which enters the novel with such disturbing effects, subverting and exceeding its ostensibly Romantic duality.

Reardon and Biffen, the putative heroes of *New Grub Street*, are both products of an old-style liberal education, attached to literature and classicism as the domain of humane values in a world of privation and struggle. Yet, although Reardon may look with nostalgia to the kind of freedom from necessity in which he imagines the 'nobly sweet hexameters' of Homer were written – 'Yes, yes; that was not written at so many pages a day, with a workhouse clock clanging its admonition at the poet's ear' (I.ix) – his own desire for such freedom is that he will no longer be required to write imaginative literature at all:

> 'If I had had the means, I should have devoted myself to the life of a scholar. That, I quite believe, is my natural

life; it's only the influence of recent circumstances that has made me a writer of novels. A man who can't journalise, yet must earn his bread by literature, nowadays inevitably turns to fiction, as the Elizabethan men turned to drama.' (I.iv, 140)

It would be too easy to devalue Reardon's critique of the commercial conditions of literary production as an escapist desire to dwell 'among the classic ghosts'. Indeed, the identification of Gissing with his hero in this respect has lent support to the fashionable myth of Gissing as a scholar whom unfortunate circumstances forced to become a writer. In fact, the classical emphasis in *New Grub Street* becomes a revelation of the paradoxical position of those intellectuals who would make literature the basis of their claims to organic status and intellectual autonomy. Romanticism, as Marilyn Butler has argued, was not merely 'a reaction against other intellectual products such as a classical style', but was more probably 'born from social experience, out of unemployment, frustration and rejection of the outside world'.[18] The social experience of Gissing's alienated, disaffected 'man of letters' has evident affinities with the fortunes of those early Romantics who had to earn a living by literature. Out of his sense of homelessness and isolation, Reardon locates in literature an organic wholeness and unity that is missing from the world; at the same time, in having to write to 'earn his bread', he lives out the contradiction between his claims to autonomy and resistance and his dependence on and submission to the market.

The central conflict, which is most tellingly revealed in Reardon's classical regret that he has to write at all, is between the spontaneous consumption of literature as the centre of human value, and its actual production, in which the Romantic conception of creative inspiration conflicts with the labour of composition and the shaping influence of the market-place. This is the real force of Marian Yule's gloomy reflections in the British Museum reading room:

One day at the end of the month she sat with books open before her, but by no effort could fix her attention upon them. It was gloomy, and one could scarcely see to read; a taste of fog grew perceptible in the warm, headachy air. Such profound discouragement possessed her that she could not even maintain the pretence of study; heedless whether anyone observed her, she let her hands fall and her head droop. She kept asking herself what was the use and purpose of such a life as she was condemned to lead. When already there was more good literature in the world than any mortal could cope with in his lifetime, here was she exhausting herself in the manufacture of printed stuff which no one even pretended to be more than a commodity for the day's market. What unspeakable folly! . . . She herself would throw away her pen with joy but for the need of earning money. And all these people about her, what aim had they save to make new books out of those already existing, that yet newer books might in turn be made out of theirs? This huge library, growing into unwieldiness, threatening to become a trackless desert of print – how intolerably it weighed upon the spirit! (I.viii, 194–5)

Critics generally interpret this passage as supporting the novel's absolute distinction between the aesthetic and the commercial value of literature. But although Marian's conception of literary culture may be absolutist and idealistic, as her references to the 'good literature' of the past make clear, her despair derives not from a Romantic aestheticism that would suppress the material basis of art, but from a nostalgic longing for material circumstances and relationships that would free the writer from the alienating conditions of commodity production in a mechanistic age.

Admittedly classicism itself does not escape ironic inspection in the novel. *New Grub Street* produces a questioning of classicism that comes close to H. G. Wells's view of Gissing's own education as

a vast collection of monumental masonry, a pale cemetery at twilight through which new conceptions hurry apologetically on their way to town, finding neither home nor sustenance there . . . which . . . can give little to life but a certain sparkle in the water and breed nothing anymore but ghosts, *ignes fatui* and infections.[19]

Yule, Reardon and Biffen are viewed as victims not simply of a mechanical society, but of an inappropriate education that has ill-equipped them for the altered conditions of the new age. In the novel, as Poole has argued, this education is seen to breed 'at best the pathetic consolation of Greek metrical effects . . . and at worst the nightmare sterility of the Yule family'.[20] There is in effect something faintly absurd about Gissing's impractical and quaintly pedantic heroes. Indeed one of the effects of the classical references in the novel is to produce an ironic contrast between the heroic world of the past and the unheroic dimensions of the contemporary world. Yet like the classical framework in Joyce's *Ulysses*, it serves not only to diminish modern man, but to locate his heroism in the seemingly unheroic experiences of an 'ignobly decent' life. This double-vision is particularly palpable in Reardon's final protracted death-bed scene, which, in a challenge to convention, combines the delirium and agonising death-struggle of the sinner of Victorian fiction with the heavenly apparitions of the saint.[21] Reardon's vision, however, is not a Christian apparition of heaven and angels, but a classical dream of Greece and the ancient glories of Actium:

> And now he stood on deck in the light of early morning. Southward lay the Ionian Islands; he looked for Ithaca, and grieved that it had been passed in the hours of darkness. But the nearest point of the main shore was a rocky promontory; it reminded him that in these waters was fought the battle of Actium.
>   The glory vanished. He lay once more a sick man in a hired chamber, longing for the dull English dawn.   (III.xxxii, 210–11)

The illusory nature of that dream is rendered with lyric force in the deadening rhythm of the final sentence. And yet Reardon's vision also suggests a return to a child-like state of innocence which recalls the death of, say, Little Nell or Catherine Earnshaw – an innocence which, however ineffectual, haunts the novel's subsequent conclusion, and stays to trouble the world that survives him. Reardon's classicism may be anachronistic, but it nevertheless exceeds the novel's own Romantic aesthetic oppositions. It is not that Gissing escapes that duality (the ideal can only have a moral victory); rather, he succeeds in producing a disturbing questioning of it.

This is particularly evident in one of the delightfully wry vignettes that contribute to the life and complexity of the novel.

It is the scene in which Reardon meets Biffen's private pupil, Mr Baker, a docker who has to 'peg away' laboriously at the difficult art of 'compersition' for the examination of the Outdoor Custom Department:

> 'There's handwriting, there's orthography, there's arithmetic; I'm not afraid of one of 'em, as Mr Biffen'll tell you, sir. But when it comes to compersition, that brings out the sweat on my forehead, I do assure you.'
>   'You're not the only man in that case, Mr Baker,' replied Reardon.
>   'It's thought a tough job in general, is it, sir?'
>   'It is indeed.'   (II.xvi, 81)

There is in the passage a traditional distinction between utility and creativity. In this context the scene would seem to provide an ironic reflection on the misuse of literature in an irredeemably mechanical age. But the self-directed irony of Reardon's response to the difficulties of the riverside man would seem to lie with equal force on the side of that reality against the illusion that literature can be separated from the social processes of production.

The sympathy of struggling writer for struggling workman at this point would seem to derive from an identification which Walter Benjamin has characterised as the 'proletarianization' of the artist.[22] It marks the establishment of a writer's solidarity with 'the people', and emerges from a recognition of his parallel situation as a worker or 'technician' within the process of the industrialisation of literary production. The novel is clearly blind to the progressive implications of this insight – the liberation of the technical means of production from the existing relations of production which are experienced by Reardon as an obstacle to creativity. The irony of the passage, and indeed the novel's whole critique, is directed against utility and technological production from a residually Romantic standpoint which would elevate the artist above the public, and above the technician. Yet the identification of the artist and the technician remains active in the novel, not only in terms of its general cultural critique, but in its directing vision of the social and material dependence of art.

It is in this respect that one can accept Mrs Leavis's claim that in the theme of authorship Gissing found a subject that was 'both inside him and outside him', without submitting to her view that the decline of literary standards was not only Gissing's passionate concern, but also a social reality. 'Literature' provided Gissing with a theme that was both inside him and outside him in so far as it involved a concretisation of a cherished ideological category of inner freedom through the motif of the 'career'. The significance of *New Grub Street* is not simply to be identified with its picture of the commercial abuses of mass literacy; nor is it to be confined to its vision of the alienating conditions of labour in an advanced industrial society. Such views have tended to emerge from and to support the equation of progress with the decline of human values, and in doing so, confuse mechanisation with its effects. Cultural decay may not lie after all in progress and the mechanisation of literary production, but in the alienating relations of production which prevent their socialisation. Gissing of course is no democrat; his intellectual perspective is essentially traditional, classical, aristocratic; yet the disparity between his idealist conception of literature and his compelling sense of its inseparability from society produces a tense and paradoxi-cal image of literary Bohemia's dependence on, and ultimate complicity with the very system it would claim to resist. The effect is a more profound questioning of social oppression and the possibilities of freedom within English society than a more narrowly liberal humanist perspective would allow.

The novel's disturbing cultural challenge lies then in the degree to which it exceeds its own Romantic humanist aesthetic. This process is not confined, however, to the exposure of the inadequacies of the ideological opposition of art and trade; it also embraces, in Gissing's representation of the life of the grub street hacks, a series of related dualisms – leisure and work, the self and the world, male and female identity – which are seen unreally to direct the total life of the individual in an age of commodity pro-duction. The scenes describing Reardon's domestic conflicts are among the most painful and powerful in the novel; they are also, significantly, the scenes of his struggles to write. The writer's life, conceived conventionally as one of integration and spontaneous, unalienated labour, serves in *New Grub Street* as a disturbing image of the breakdown of the conventional division of free family rela-tionships and compulsory labour. Here, for instance, is a charac-teristically exhaustive description of the multiplying tensions and inconveniences caused by Reardon's presence in the home:

Under the best of circumstances it was awkward to receive any but intimate friends during the hours when Reardon sat at his desk. The little dining-room (with its screen to conceal the kitchen range) offered nothing more than homely comfort; and then the servant had to be disposed of by sending her into the bedroom to take care of Willie. Privacy, in the strict sense, was impossible, for the servant might listen at the door (one room led out of the other) to all the conversation that went on; yet Amy could not request her visitors to speak in a low tone. For the first year these difficulties had not been felt; Reardon had made a point of leaving the front room at his wife's disposal from three to six; it was only when dread of the future began to press upon him, that he sat in the study all day long. You see how complicated were the miseries of the situation; one torment involved another, and in every quarter subjects of discontent were multiplied.   (I.x, 247)

It is a situation which links the violence and oppressions of private life to the patterns of domination and struggle in society as a whole.

One finds a similar image of the interpenetration of work and home in D. H. Lawrence's *Sons and Lovers*, where, as Terry Eagleton has argued, Morel is a reflection of a dominative society as it reaches into the offered alternatives of free family relationships.[23] There are significant differences: Reardon, unlike Morel, is unable to adopt the masculine postures of brute force and sexual domination either in the world of work *or* in the world of home. Indeed, it is to this 'natural' violence and domination that the infuriatingly conventional Amy would goad him:

He had but to do one thing: to seize her by the arm, drag her up from the chair, dash her back again with all his force – there, and the transformation would be complete, they would stand towards each other on the natural footing. With the added curse perhaps –

Instead of that, he choked, struggled for breath and shed tears.

Amy turned scornfully away from him. Blows and a curse would have overawed her, at all events for the moment; she would have felt: 'Yes, he is a man, and I have put my destiny into his hands.' His tears moved her to feel cruelly exultant; they were the sign of her superiority. It was she who should have wept, and never in her life had she been further from such display of weakness. (II.xvii, 118)

Reardon's unmanly tears; his refusal to demand obedience and subservience from his wife: these very weaknesses are a form of resistance and refusal of those conventionally sanctioned roles for men and women which Amy unquestioningly accepts. Indeed it is in these terms that Reardon accuses her at their bitter parting: 'You helped me in nothing. You threw all the responsibility upon me – always bearing in mind, I suppose, that there was a refuge for you' (II.xvii). It is not that Reardon renounces the traditional notions of sexual hierarchy. After his separation from Amy, he indulges in male fantasies of marriage to 'some simple, kind-hearted work-girl' (III.xxvii). It is simply that the claim for masculine authority is seen to have no binding force in the socially and economically insecure world of lower middle-class life where the only law is the struggle for survival. This feeling is expressed most vividly in Reardon's 'bitterness at his lot' as he hears the bells of St Marylebone clang for afternoon service, and reflects that the 'world might be a sufficing paradise to him if only he could clutch a poor little share of current coin. He had won the world's greatest prize – a woman's love – but he could not retain it because his pockets were empty' (II.xvii).

In *New Grub Street*, as in *Sons and Lovers*, there are also moments of domestic tenderness and relaxation. The happiness of the family when Morel has work to do in the house is matched in *New Grub Street* by those soothing moments when Reardon reads to Amy from his cherished Homer. It is significant, however, that whereas Morel's infectious humour results from bringing his skills as a good workman into the home, moments 'when he was his real self again', Reardon's happiness depends on a show of learning that displays more completely his estrangement from those practical matters which his occasionally indulgent, but never wholly sympathetic wife keeps constantly in view. His moments of joy become an occasion not of unity and harmony, but of threatened conflict, estrangement and reproach. For Reardon, as for Morel, the family is not an alternative to the restrictions of work, but a new set of limiting relationships – both men, for example, feel Oedipal rivalry towards their sons in their struggle to possess the mother's love – yet, in the life of Reardon the writer, the breakdown between the free family and the bondage of work is in the end more complete.

It is for this reason that Reardon in paradoxical manner retreats 'back to obscurity' as 'a harmless clerk, a decent wage earner' (II.xix). His motives are not simply practical. Indeed there is something grotesque and irrational in the euphoria with which Reardon sheds his family home, his furniture, his material possessions. In the break-up of Reardon's marriage, Gissing renders with painful accuracy and acute insight the irreconcilable conflicts and estrangements of those inadequately conventional expectations by which men and women judge each other. As the finely repressed strains of Gissing's dialogue make clear, Reardon's separation from Amy is, on one level, a refusal to act to the traditional male role: 'I will have no woman slave dragging out a weary life with me', he announces in tragic, self-congratulatory tones during their final 'fruitless meeting' (III.xxv). At the same time, his retreat from family life also involves an irrational longing to re-establish a consolatory division between the self and the world, between free relationship and compulsory labour whose abstraction the novel has already exposed. It is this which deprives Reardon's appeal to essential selfhood of any persuasive force – 'Don't you think of me apart from all that I may do or not do? If I had to earn my living as a clerk, would that make me a clerk in soul?' (II.xv). His demand is for Amy's unconditional love and unqualified devotion to who he is, and not what he does. Admittedly Amy is far from being a noble or exemplary type, and the terms of her refusal betray a certain moral and intellectual inadequacy – 'I am certainly not the wife of a clerk who is paid so much a week' (II.xvii) – but the tyranny of the contractual sacrifice demanded of her is one which the level-headed and self-respecting Amy must with some justice reject.

There is in the end no authority granted to Reardon's stubborn idealism. The patterns of the plot which ultimately transfer wife, wealth and reputation from Reardon, the perverse self-pitying idealist, to Milvain, the practical opportunistic friend of the family, would seem to ratify Milvain's own rationalistic belief in the survival of the fittest. 'To say that nothing in the novel opposes Milvain's rationality', as John Goode has argued, 'is to put it too mildly . . . Reardon's whole story depends on his tacit acquiescence in Milvain's world view . . . his [Milvain's] rationality effectively becomes the novel's reality.'[24] This would seem to apply with particular force to the representation of love, which, like literature, is here denied the kind of romantic exemption from the determinations of social life which it conventionally enjoys. Milvain characteristically objects to the word 'love' altogether:

'It has been vulgarized. Let us talk about compatibility. Now, I should say that, no doubt, and speaking scientifically, there *is* one particular woman supremely fitted to each man . . . The days of romantic love are gone by. The scientific spirit has put an end to that kind of self-deception . . . What we think of now is moral and intellectual and physical compatibility; I mean, if we are reasonable people.' (II.xxii, 262–3)

Milvain ruthlessly applies his anti-romantic principles in his courtship of Marian Yule and ultimate choice of Amy. For insensitivity and near comic absurdity, Milvain's courtship of Marian comes close to matching Bertie Stanhope's grotesque offer of marriage to Mrs Bold in Trollope's *Barchester Towers*. It is clear, however, that Milvain is not to be viewed as either a villain or a fool. His rationality and energetic optimism make him at one with his environment and ultimately with the novel's own Social Darwinian perspective. It is for this reason that the attempt to separate the marriage theme from the 'amalgam of realistically conceived environment' results in a severe distortion of the novel.[25] For such a reading rests implicitly on the assumption that matters of personal life in, say, love and marriage are *a priori* 'free' and independent of external social structures.

The novel's own divergence from this view is given tragic dimension in Marian's struggle between love and duty. For Marian's choice *as a woman* is not between the absolute freedoms of marriage and the bondage of her paternal home, but between two sets of limiting relationships. Indeed her toil in the literary market-place as her father's 'work-horse' gives her a tragic dignity and independence denied to the wholly domestic Amy. It is a conflict that Gissing will go on to explore in his subsequent novels – notably in *In the Year of Jubilee* and *The Whirlpool*. In *New Grub Street*, love can claim no absolute moral sanction. Rather, Marian, with the fine instincts of a daughter who has had to mediate between a disappointed father and a dependent, querulous mother, tries heroically to reconcile the responsibilities of personal fulfilment and filial loyalty until the loss of her legacy deprives her of any margin of release.

In the end Marian's fate would also seem to endorse Milvain's cruelly patronising view of individual failure and the survival of the fittest. And yet the novel cannot be said morally to support the scientific view. Although rationality is offered as an ideological reflection of an environment of struggle and scarcity in which inner resistance is finally ineffectual, that resistance remains active, an irrational refusal of a corrupt and morally vacuous social order whose laws are accepted paradoxically as absolute. It is this which compels Jasper's own candid admission that in terms of literary value, his productions are 'equal to that of the contents of a mouldy nut' (II.xiv). His frank acceptance of his literary char-latanism is all of a piece with his confessions of moral conscience. 'I shall do many a base thing in life', he warns Marian, 'just to get money and reputation; I tell you this that you mayn't be surprised if anything of that kind comes to your ears. I can't afford to live as I should like to' (I.viii). While conceding to the absolute demands of economic necessity, Jasper nevertheless registers a moral self-rebuke. 'There is', he claims, 'the man apart from his necessities.' The reader is urged here not to endorse Milvain's unconscious idealism, but to recognise the irony of the novel's double refusal of withdrawal and absorption, of the kind of failure that is absolute and the kind of success that represents moral failure.

This is the real force of the narrator's interventionist pleading on behalf of Reardon and Biffen in the third volume of the novel:

> The chances are that you have neither understanding nor sympathy for such men as Edwin Reardon and Harold Biffen. They merely provoke you. They seem to you inert, flabby, weakly envious, foolishly obstinate, impiously mutinous, and many other things. You are made angrily contemptuous of their failure to get on; why don't they bestir themselves, push and bustle, welcome kicks so long as a halfpence follow, make a place in the world's eye – in short, take a leaf from the book of Mr Jasper Milvain?
> But try to imagine a personality wholly unfitted for the rough and tumble of the world's labour-market. From the familiar point of view these men were worthless; view them in possible relation to a humane order of society, and they are admirable citizens. Nothing is easier than to condemn a type of character which is unequal to the coarse demands of life as it suits the average man. These two were richly endowed with the kindly

and imaginative virtues; if fate threw them amid incongruous circumstances, is their endowment of less value? You scorn their passivity; but it was their nature and their merit to be passive. Gifted with independent means, each of them would have taken quite a different aspect in your eyes. The sum of their faults was their inability to earn money; but, indeed, that inability does not call for unmingled disdain. (III.xxxi, 168–9)

It is a passage in which the author, in Goode's view, 'seems to be compensating for the disintegration of the fictional structure'.[26] Yet the view that their value and merit lies in their failure in an inhumane society is insufficiently understood if it is seen simply as a defence of idealism and attempted reaffirmation of the already demystified preserve of inner emigration and heroic selfhood. Rather it is an appeal for a transformation of material circumstances – what Gissing refers to as the 'possible relation to a humane order of society' – which would support the ideal of organic culture.

This is the source of that contradiction which critics have noted in Gissing's work. It takes the form of a shift from the explanation of the failure of his favoured characters in terms of an inhumane social order to an identification of their failure simply with lack of money. Whereas the former suggests protest and the need for change, the latter indicates an acceptance of existing social organisation. Money is seen as a potential solution to the separation of inner and outer worlds. Yet whereas the residually sentimental and melodramatic structure of the early novels tends to provide a means of preserving the Arnoldian ideal, in *New Grub Street* that mythological solution is significantly refused. Here, as in *The Nether World*, the Victorian legacy plot is a nakedly anti-Romantic device, a tragicomic vehicle for the display of avarice and grotesque delusions in the lower-class world of scarcity and struggle.

The fortune which finally falls to Amy does not in fact resolve Reardon's difficulties. The reason for his refusal to return to Amy and 'life without struggle' is not simply his wounded sense that she no longer loves him, but that money alone cannot heal the hidden injuries of those who, through 'accursed poverty', have seen too deeply into the heart of a society which is base and brutal (III.xxvii). Dignity, for Reardon, can only be achieved by withdrawal. It is this which to some extent resolves the seeming discrepancy in the novel between the view that money can have a humanising and ennobling effect, supporting spacious culture, and the controlling thesis of cultural and moral degeneration which shapes its final vision of the philistine sufficiency of Jasper and Amy's literary coterie. Though money may provide an escape from 'the struggle against destitution', 'independent means' does not in the end provide a genuine alternative to the inadequacies of withdrawal and absorption. The novel in effect exposes the illusion of its own ideological wish. 'And they are empty creatures who live there', is Amy's response to Reardon's envious vision of the rich earlier in the novel in what might be an ironic footnote to her own 'happy ending'. Amy intuitively recognises the externality of such a life. Yet in asking Reardon to return to her, she also realises that he would more likely 'lapse into a life of scholarly self indulgence, such as he had often told her was his ideal' (III.xxvi). The novel, through the 'typical woman of the new time, the woman who has developed concurrently with the journalistic enterprise', is made with fitting irony to register the inadequacy of the two men who in turn possess her. What the reader is confronted with in the end is a double refusal of the self and society that not only resists the degraded present, but with reluctant and disturbing insight throws into relief the fundamental complicity of traditional, idealistic resolves.

5

The Refusal of Irony:
Born in Exile

Wandering between two worlds, one dead,
The other powerless to be born.

Matthew Arnold

Begun before the proofs of *New Grub Street* had been completed, *Born in Exile* focuses with new intensity on the problem of intellectual freedom and autonomy in modern English life. Appropriately in a novel which sets out to explore the residual anachronism of English cultural class formations, it is the sight of an 'aristocratic' carriage in Hyde Park which becomes the occasion of the hero's formulation of his purpose and ambition:

> Close in front of him an open carriage came to a stop; in it sat, or rather reclined, two ladies, old and young. Upon this picture Godwin fixed his eyes with the intensity of fascination; his memory never lost the impress of these ladies' faces. . . . Here he stood, one of the multitude, one of the herd; shoulder to shoulder with boors and pickpockets; and within reach of his hand reposed those two ladies, in Olympian calm, seeming unaware even of the existence of the throng. . . . They were his equals, those ladies, merely his equals. With such as they he should by right of nature associate. (II.ii, 129)

It is a scene that recalls Reardon's sight of the rich man's carriage in *New Grub Street*; but whereas for Reardon the carriage is a reminder of his exclusion and difference that is finally demoralising, for the hero of the later novel it produces a moment of 'passionate perception' that fixes his desire. His Olympian vision is conceived not simply in terms of wealth; it embraces an absolute sense of class. His desire to scale the social heights to which he feels he belongs 'by right of nature' takes the form of an overmastering ambition to marry a woman of perfect breeding.

In spite of its English preoccupations, *Born in Exile* is a masterly rendering of the complexities of nineteenth-century intellectual life which claims an undeniable place next to *New Grub Street* in the corpus of Gissing's work. It is a novel which, in Walter Allen's view, 'reveals Gissing as a man who has profited by and made his own some of the most revolutionary ideas of his time, ideas which, embodied in the character and behaviour of Peak, link the novel with European masterpieces'.[1] This conception of the novel has in the past found a more general critical acceptance outside England. American and Continental critics have in this respect been more responsive than their English counterparts to the pathos and irony of Peak's situation. Jacob Korg, for instance, in a seminal essay, links *Born in Exile* with other European 'masterpieces' of the period, notably with Dostoevsky's *Crime and Punishment*, Turgenev's *Fathers and Sons* and Jacobsen's *Niels Lyhne*, as an expression of a general crisis of spiritual and intellectual unrest.[2] The novel is judged in this view to be an exemplary story of the aridity and inevitable failure of the nineteenth-century scientific ideal. Pierre Coustillas, who closely follows Korg's reading, has gone so far as to see in the novel's final position 'a form of "lay humanism" in which Gissing comes, through the dissection of his past errors, to admit the "vanity of revolt"'.[3]

Though English readers have responded favourably to the novel's disturbing intellectual force, their attitude has tended to include an element of formal and ethical complaint, not to say embarrassment, at Gissing's *lack of irony* towards his hero's ludicrous ambition to marry a 'lady'. 'It is clear,' writes Frank Swinnerton, in a generally favourable account of the novel, 'that Peak's desire for a life of supra-refinement, grotesque though it is, has the author's serious approval; the book is for this reason humourless.'[4] Like Swinnerton, English critics are in general alienated by Gissing's failure to render with adequate irony what they feel to be Peak's unattractive and sometimes ludicrous snobbery. There would seem to be a curious contradiction here between those who celebrate the presence of irony in the novel, and those who regret its absence. Yet one might notice, on the part of both sets of readers, an acceptance of the need for aesthetic privilege and self-exemption. The aim of the present reading will be to show that ironic detachment is in fact conspicuously absent from the novel; the narrator may recognise that Peak has set himself upon a fool's errand, but it is in terms which continue to identify with his aspirations. Yet to admit the justice of Swinnerton's view and that of Gissing's English readers generally is not to submit to their aesthetic judgement. Indeed it will be shown that the novel's lack of ironic detachment is the very basis of its power and effectivity in making visible the social and cultural imperatives of Peak's seemingly absurd and irrational behaviour. Not the least disturbing of the novel's unique effects is its exposure, in the specific context of English class formations, of the evident evasions and complicity which liberal humanist claims for freedom and self-exemption would seem to involve. Gissing, as John Goode has pointed out,

> cares too much about the existential nakedness of the situation he portrays to worry too much about the possessive sensibilities of his . . . readers. You cannot read a Gissing novel in terms of a liberal morality because there is always more going on than such an abstraction allows for.[5]

It is significant that those who have sought a moral perspective within the novel here tended to locate it in the character of Earwaker.[6] Although the novel gently mocks Bohemian ideals – notably the wealthy Malkin's exuberant cosmopolitan independence of conventional society, and the 'singularity' of the orphaned Moxeys with their fixation for 'sympathetic companions' – Earwaker would seem to represent the possibility of combining intellectual resistance and social success. Yet it is significant that such a possibility is only allowed within a broader structure of representation that finally reveals the unheroic nature of Earwaker's measure of radicalism and common sense.

This qualification is registered with greatest force at the moment of Peak's anguished defence of the individual's right to defy conscience, following the failure of his scheme to marry the pure and delicate Sidwell Warricombe, the sister of a former college friend, by posing as a clergyman-to-be. Earwaker's generous belief that his friend will one day no longer have to look at life through 'preposterous sexual spectacles' is matched by the narrator's own final verdict on Earwaker which is at that moment equally damning in its generosity:

> Earwaker had his place in the social system, his growing circle of friends, his congenial labour. . . . All this with no sacrifice of principle. He was fortunate in his temper, moral and intellectual; partly directing circumstances, partly guided by their pressure, he advanced on the way of harmonious development. Nothing great would come of his endeavours, but what he aimed at he steadily perfected. . . . Nature had been kind to him; what more could one say? (VI.iii, 443)

The lack of heroism that attends Earwaker's fortunate advance to his 'place in the social system' lies not so much in his compromise with the reality of struggle. This after all involves no 'sacrifice of principle'. It lies in his basic inability, or temperamental unwillingness to interrogate the ambivalent areas of moral superstition on which the system rests. Peak too devotes himself to science and radical journalism as possible channels of social influence and personal success, but this yields in the end to a recognition of the inevitable inferiority of such efforts. Faced with the reality of entrenched social stratification, Peak transfers his energies from London and the contentions of urban life to the leisured world of rank and privilege. 'Put it in the correct terms', he confesses to Earwaker, 'I am a plebeian, and I aim at marrying a lady' (II.ii).

Yet Peak's perspective remains unequivocally modern. Driven by the social aspirations and financial insecurities of his class to 'fight the world with his brains', educated among the sons of 'the robust employers of labour' who 'were for the most part avowed Radicals, in theory scornful of privilege', Peak's outlook on life is one of scientific rationalism and the survival of the fittest. The novel registers in effect a fundamental disjunction in English life; for while the social system remains actively aristocratic, in an ideological sense at least, the prevailing conditions of existence are directed by economic individualism which emphasises 'careerism' as a means of validating worth. It is this opposition which gives birth to the novel's complex and interrelated levels of discourse; one involves Peak's intellectual challenge to moral and metaphysical presuppositions; the other, the imperatives of social mobility as a means of personal validation. It also produces the central paradox or contradiction inherent in Peak's attempt to infiltrate the sanctity of the upper middle-classs household by exploiting Warricombe's belated hope of reconciling rationalism and religion.

In this Peak's duplicity differs fundamentally from the meretricious adjustments of Bruno Chilvers, his rival for Sidwell's love. Chilvers combines religious orthodoxy and frank materialism without any deep betrayal of his social allegiances or his personal integrity. His externality corresponds to the theatricality of Dickens's comic types, functioning both as satirical device and as a register of his capacity for survival in an individualistic age still dominated by moral formulae.[7] Yet the point about Chilvers is that unlike his Dickensian counterpart, he has no real claim to 'typicality'; Chilvers is himself part of the already consolidated upper stratum of English society. It is a formation which the established religion sustains, and from which it draws its recruits. He is motivated by vanity and egoism, but whether this operates 'to make a cleric of a secret materialist, or to incite a display of excessive liberalism in one whose convictions were orthodox' – Peak significantly prefers 'the latter surmise' (V.i) – his integrity remains intact:

> He trod in the footsteps of his father, and with inherited aptitude moulded antique traditions into harmony with the taste of the times. (III.iv, 260)

Chilvers is introduced into the novel as a satirical representation of the 'organic' bourgeois intellectual of the English type. His latitudinarian attempt to reconcile progress and ethical demand constitutes a characteristic philosophical pragmatism aimed at smoothing the way towards a secular 'bourgeois' culture. Born lower down the social scale, Peak manifests the problematic condition of the new 'traditional' intellectual anomalously created within the increasingly corporate structures of late-Victorian capitalism.

It is worth stressing that the anomalies of this situation are not simply to be seen as the idiosyncratic concern of Gissing's hero in *Born in Exile*. Their influence can be traced in the changing structures of the late-Victorian novel generally. There is a marked contrast, for instance, between the triumph of the lower middle-class hero of *David Copperfield* and the picture of social and intellectual disillusionment that closes Dickens's original ending of *Great Expectations*. It is the discrepancy between the dream of transcendence that underpins the *déclassé* motif of the classic realist novel, and the reality of frustration that is the experience of life in the increasingly specialised world of late-Victorian capitalism. For both Peak and Pip, the obstacles to becoming a gentleman are no longer the merely external ones of speech and deportment. Both heroes are granted the kind of patronage and education that facilitates social mobility. Rather, their problem is rooted in their adherence to an aristocratic ideal in a world of expanding desires and narrowing opportunities. It is a world in which they must not only renounce their inferior origins – this is seen in both novels to involve its own pattern of guilt – but in which they must also preserve their hidden ideal from their own guilty assault. Peak articulates this dilemma in terms of a double refusal:

> 'Whether I remained with my kith and kin, or turned my back upon them in the hope of finding my equals, I was condemned to a life of miserable incompleteness. I was born in exile.'   (V.ii, 363)

Ideologically tied to an organic conception of society that is not only backward looking, but emphatically aristocratic, Peak is finally unable to voice the genuine conceptual theory that his grand claims for belonging 'by right of intellect' inchoately strives for. But further than that, he is compelled to safeguard the very institutions which ensure his continuing sense of inauthenticity and exclusion. He remains an exile in his own kingdom.

Peak's violation of the Warricombe house is accompanied by feelings of deference as well as of scorn, exhibiting all the 'emotional ambivalence' which Freud was to associate with the active social stricture of 'taboo', and in particular with that conflict between solicitude and hostility characteristic of people's attitude to rulers and 'privileged persons':

> alongside of the veneration, and indeed idealization, felt towards them, there is in the unconscious an opposing current of intense hostility . . . in fact . . . we are faced with a situation of emotional ambivalence.[8]

It is clear in this connection that we are not meant to see Peak simply as someone who has sacrificed his moral and intellectual integrity for the sake of social advancement. Peak is caught in a double-bind. He is committed not only to the demands of rationalism and self-validation, with their necessary refusal of the sacred institutions of rank and privilege, but also to a still-active veneration for those very institutions.

That this 'emotional ambivalence' is to some extent shared by the author is evident in the tensions of the narrative discourse itself. The conflict between 'hypocrisy' and 'ungenerous irony', between snobbish reverence and intellectual scorn, which Peak experiences in the Warricombe household, is to be felt in the novel's opening account of prize-giving day at Whitelaw College. Stiff, latinate, drained of all exuberance: the inhibitions of the narrator's own ironic detachment from the 'boundless self-satisfaction' of the rich and privileged would seem to derive from the same insecurities as Peak's ambiguous envy and self-doubt. This is also palpable in the early scenes of the novel in which we see Peak turn his back, first on his family, and then on the fellowship of Bohemian London. The account of Peak's encounter with his Cockney uncle is particularly disturbing in its refusal of an exemptive or comforting laughter. Andrew Peak's unashamed vulgarity in planning to open an eating-house opposite his nephew's college clearly promises an energetic challenge to the hero's aristocratic hauteur. The disproportionate horror produced by his brief but extravagant appearance at the Peak family home suggests all the possibility of Dickensian satire and comic deflation. Indeed the novel itself would seem to entertain such possibilities when Peak is made to wonder whether his uncle is 'wholly unconscious of the misery he was causing' (I.iii). But these possibilities are admitted only to be refused. Though there is clearly a hint of resentment and ridicule in Andrew Peak's obtrusive coarseness, he nevertheless accepts the superiority of his educated relatives. In encouraging his son Jowey's phonetic massacre of 'The Rime of the Ancient Mariner', his desire is for association and emulation. If aggressive self-esteem results here in buffoonery and self-humiliation, the roots of that gaucherie are nevertheless to be traced to the same hidden injuries of class that direct the hero's 'coward delicacy' and ultimately divert all irony from his protective stratagems.

Like the hero of *Crime and Punishment*, to whom he clearly bears a close fictional resemblance, Peak is driven to violate society's law in the name of rationalism and his own sovereign will. His compulsion is rooted in the same ambivalent impulse which bears within it the opposing need to punish himself for his transgression. Violation brings about its own internal Nemesis. The simultaneous ascendancy of wish and counter-wish compels both heroes into oscillating fits of exhilaration and self-loathing, of pride and dread, that ultimately threaten their sanity. In his colloquy with Sidwell's father, subduing 'the impulses of disrespect', Peak experiences the same 'tormenting metaphysical doubt of his own identity' which infects Raskolnikov during his meetings with Porfiry Petrovitch, the police interrogator. Dostoevsky's protrayal of eruptive demonism is here recoverable in Gissing's account of his hero's metaphysical anguish and loss of self:

> With involuntary attempt to recover the familiar self he grasped his own wrist, and then, before he was aware, a laugh escaped him, an all but mocking laugh.   (III.iv, 252)

and:

> Often enough the debates were perilously suggestive of burlesque, and, when alone, he relieved himself of the laughter he had scarce restrained.   (III.iv, 253)

Such passages have a parodic ring. And yet, although *Born in Exile* is clearly modelled on *Crime and Punishment*, the drama of transgression and internal Nemesis is unequivocally located in Gissing's novel in the specifically social imperatives and determinations of class conflict.

Peak's deliberate lie comes significantly after a whole series of minor deceptions dictated principally by the need to conceal his humble origins. This compulsion not only directs his departure from Whitelaw; it also constrains him to conceal his true reason for going. His subsequent chance encounters with his former school-fellows are in turn fraught with an embarrassed reticence about the past. Peak's evasions are directed, as Adrian Poole has suggested, by a fear of exposure that would 'destroy the illusion of perfect inner chastity';[9] but that very illusion is itself rooted in the need to maintain a sense of autonomy and worth in the face of a rigidly stratified society. Moreover the tact displayed by Earwaker and the Warricombes indicates that Peak's class anxieties are not simply idiosyncratic:

That deep-rooted sense of class which had so much influence on his speculative and practical life asserted itself,. with rigid consistency, even against his own aspirations. . . . He, it was true, belonged to no class whatever, acknowledged no subordination save that of the hierarchy of intelligence; but this could not obscure the fact that his brother sold seeds across a counter, that his sister had married a haberdasher. (III.iv, 246)

The 'lie' itself is acted out 'without premeditation, almost without consciousness . . . under the marvelling regard of his conscious self' (II.iii). Peak, in refusing to confess to a 'base motive', comes to account for it in terms of a moral compulsion, in which morality itself is firmly rooted in social constraint:

'An opportunity offered of achieving the supreme end to which my life is directed, and what scruple could stand in my way? We have nothing to do with names and epithets. *Here* are the facts of life as I had known it; *there* is the existence promised as the reward of successful artifice. To live was to pursue the object of my being. I could not feel otherwise; therefore, could not act otherwise.' (VI.iii, 439)

In transferring the burden of guilt to 'the society that compelled to such an expedient', Peak recognises the 'profound moral crisis' underlying his compulsion (II.iv). His actions, like those of Raskolnikov, are seen on one level to spring from a frustrated sense of worth in a residually traditional society deeply infected with the imperatives of personal validation. Peak justifies his 'simulated orthodoxy' in terms of a need to satisfy his 'craving for love capable only of a social (one might say, of a political) definition' (III.ii). His extenuation here embraces not only the trauma of inner worth, but the need to sustain and reassure the old order against the threat of democratic extension of which he paradoxically is a part. Indeed the heroes of both novels, in their different social and cultural contexts, can be seen to represent an intellectual challenge to the moral and ideological insufficiency of nineteenth-century liberal 'bourgeois' doctrines. Yet whereas Raskolnikov seeks nothing less than the destruction of the established order in clearing the ground for a new and better society, Peak pursues a naïve and regressive ideal of integrating with the old order.

It is a difference which reflects not only the restrictions of mind, but also the compelling insights that result from the special nature of English ideological class formations. There is in *Born in Exile* no Dostoevskian appeal to sacrifice as an ethical solution to the social and historical crisis which is seen to underlie the hero's transgression and loss of self. In *Born in Exile* the social origins of Peak's anguish remain on show in all their contradiction. At the same time Gissing's novel admits nothing of that margin of freedom for the mind which resonates with future promise in Dostoevsky's account of a similar intellectual rebellion. *Crime and Punishment* may seem to be conservative and reactionary in its final appeal to authority and necessary submission, but it is clear, as Nicholas Berdyaev has argued, that Dostoevsky 'saw no possibility of a return to the conception of life, a static and immovable form, that existed before the arising of the revolutionary spirit'.[10] In spite of his inherent conservatism, Dostoevsky's critique of the present is rooted in the same progressive intellectual utopianism to which the hero gives voice. By contrast *Born in Exile* shows its hero in irresistible bondage to traditional intellectual categories that allow no such autonomy for the life of the mind.

This is true not only of Peak, but of those who judge him. Buckland Warricombe may recognise the difficulties of alloting moral blame in an angular age still dominated by traditional pieties:

> There's that fellow Bruno Chilvers: mightn't anyone who had personal reasons treat him precisely as I have treated Peak? Both of them *may* be honest. Yet in Peak's case all appearances are against him – just because he is of low birth, has no means, and wants desperately to get into society. The fellow is a scoundrel; I am convinced of it. Yet his designs may be innocent. How, then, a scoundrel? (V.iii, 375)

The question 'How, then, a scoundrel?' is one that he himself has already answered. The final derogatory epithet echoes Peak's own explanation of Warricombe's 'determined anger': 'personal motives have made you regard me as – a scoundrel'. Moral indignation is here seen to be an ally of class prejudice. Moreover, though Sidwell herself is more forgiving on discovering 'the dishonourable part he had played', Peak recognises that she had been able to disregard his low origins 'only because of what she had then deemed his spiritual value' (V.iv). Both Sidwell's 'natural prejudice' and Peak's 'apology for his transgression' are rooted equally in the imperatives of class. Even though the novel registers the naïvety of Peak's attempt to turn back the clock – Sidwell's gradual drift 'further and further from the old religion', for instance, would seem in the end to discount his whole enterprise as 'superfluous' – it continues to recognise the dominance of those sanctions which compels Peak to preserve the old world from his own assault, and to refuse what he has won. Indeed it is for this reason that Sidwell's final grandiloquent appeal to Peak to fight for his place 'in the new order . . . with men who are working for the future' is not only irrelevant, but almost wilfully disingenuous. For the 'modern intellectual life' to which she directs him is precisely the one which her own jealously guarded 'little world' renders socially and ideologically subservient.

The novel makes telling allusion in this context to Browning's 'Waring'. The situation of the poem is suggestively woven into the narrative's richly intertextual structure – the high claims for great works undone that attended a frustrated sense of worth; the sudden mysterious desertion of London and old friends; the fantastic speculations and sightings that such a disappearance produces. The irony of Browning's poem is directed, by the force of the dramatic monologue itself, against the latent frustration and exilic loneliness of Bohemian London. It is an alienation which the monologuist's obsession unconsciously reveals. The experience of London is itself exile, and in particular the conditions of modern intellectual life which produce a *malaise* in the heart of the young man of the new order 'hungry for acknowledgement'. By turning back to the old order, Peak may have condemned himself to a 'wasted life', but the sense of exile which has prompted him reaches more deeply into the ideological heartlands of history than Sidwell's ingenuous exhortation would allow. For Peak's 'exile' engages the whole problematic question of intellectual independence and personal worth in an advanced industrial society still 'in fealty to' an uncontested traditionalism. It is this conflict – neither reduced nor superseded – which Peak bears back with him, first to London, and then, a ghostly homeless wanderer, to his death 'in exile'.

Peak remains for this reason an enigma to the end. The photograph which Earwaker inserts with 'a curious sense of satisfaction' in his album is of 'a face by which every intelligent eye must be arrested; which no two observers would interpret in the same way' (VII.i). On one level the scene suggests Bohemia's guilty fascination for one who has refused its repressions and compromises; but equally it bears out the whole import of the novel that to 'interpret' Peak at all is in a sense to evade the social contradictions that he embodies.

And yet, if the novel itself makes no attempt to 'resolve' the enigmatic and finally undecidable nature of Peak's character and behaviour, readers have in general been less inhibited. The response of critics outside England has on the whole been more generous in this respect. Their view of the novel as an ironic study of nineteenth-century intellectual revolt tends, however, not only to acquiesce in the very metaphysical assumptions the novel would have us question, but to obscure its specifically 'English' elements. Indeed one suspects that their generosity is in the end the margin of their own intellectual privilege applied to the novel, a margin of freedom for the life of the mind which neither Peak, nor his creator, nor indeed his English critics, possess.

6

Oddness and Typicality:
The Odd Women

> It is the problem of today, the establishment
> of a new relation, or the readjustment of the
> old one, between man and woman.
>
> D. H. Lawrence

In a letter written to his German friend, Eduard Bertz, in February 1892, Gissing outlined his plans for a new novel:

> The book I now have in mind is to deal with the great question of 'throwing pearls before swine'. It will present those people who, congenitally incapable of true education, have yet been taught to consider themselves too good for manual, or any humble, work. As yet I have chiefly dealt with types expressing the struggles of nature endowed *above* their station; now I turn to those who are *below* it. The story will be a study of vulgarism – the all but triumphant force of our time. Women will be the chief characters.[1]

It is generally assumed that the passage refers to *The Odd Women* which Gissing completed after a long struggle in October that year. Indeed this has become the basis of an influential interpretation of the novel which would link it with *In the Year of Jubilee* and *The Whirlpool* as a 'study in vulgarism'.[2] Yet to review the evidence of Gissing's long and difficult struggle that year to begin his new novel is to become aware of an altogether more problematic beginning for *The Odd Women* than this would suggest.

Gissing was in fact to write to Bertz eleven times that year, his correspondence indicating alternate moods of exhilaration and frustration. As early as March, for instance, he was to confess to having abandoned his original intention: 'After all, my new book will not be what I said. I am still groping about.'[3] In May, however, although frustrated by his inability to find a title for his new book, he seems to have reverted to his original theme, and the tone is again scathing and assured:

I want to deal with the flood of blackguardism which nowadays is pouring forth over the society which is reared by wealth above the lowest and yet not sufficiently educated to rank with the highest. Impossible to take up the newspaper nowadays without being impressed by this fact of extending and deepening vulgarity.[4]

A month later he is again 'out of sorts' and 'working slowly and with perpetual alteration'.[5] In representing himself to Bertz as progressing steadily if slowly on a single project, Gissing is not being entirely honest, and confessed as much when, in the calm that followed the completion of *The Odd Women*, he was to speak candidly of having concealed the real struggle of composition.[6] His is a writer's natural reticence, and is directed, one suspects, by the need to sustain his own fragile faith in unrealised projects, as well as by the need to spare others the truth about literary composition. A despairing diary entry of 1 July reveals the truth: 'On looking back I see that the novel I have now begun is the *seventh* attempt since my last [*Denzil Quarrier*] was finished. Each time a new subject. Something wrong here.'[7]

The real change in Gissing's mood comes, however, at the beginning of August. 'The summer,' he writes to Bertz,

has, for me, been all but wasted. I have begun several stories, but in each case only to destroy what I wrote. Now, after a holiday, I am again making a beginning, and I think with better hope. I must get a book done so as to have some money before the end of the year.[8]

A day on his own at the seaside resort of Seaton on the south coast appears to have provided the inspiration for 'an entirely new story'.[9] It is significant that the new novel is no longer referred to in strident Carlylean terms; it is being written simply 'to have some money'. Although Gissing was to have one more new start,[10] he had completed volume one by the end of August, and confidently states his theme to Bertz in tones very different from his original project: 'It deals with women who, from a marriage point of view, are *superfluous*. "The Odd Women" I shall perhaps call it.'[11] That Gissing did not associate *The Odd Women* with his earlier plan is further supported by his surprise after publication that critics should insist upon its 'absorbing interest'.[12] Though for Gissing readers it has always been considered among his best works, for Gissing himself it was written simply to earn money. *The Odd Women* can in fact be linked to his initial Carlylean intention to the extent that all of his major works show concern for the manifestations of general cultural decline. The conscious linking of 'liberationist' ideals with the 'fact of extending and deepening vulgarity', however, is to be found in two later novels – *In the Year of Jubilee* and *The Whirlpool* – which explore the effects of sham education and culture on the lives of women.

In its exploration of topical feminist issues and the possibility of new relationship between men and women, *The Odd Women* has a different centre of interest. The investigation of marriage and woman's role in society is a central feature of Gissing's work from the first, and indeed of the mid- and late-Victorian novel generally. What Gissing does in *The Odd Women* is to find a specific historical focus for that thematic interest in contemporary feminist debate. 'The major feminine characters', as Jacob Korg has pointed out, 'are notable examples of Gissing's ability to dramatize the interplay of social forces and individual psychology.'[13] Gissing had in fact tried earlier to link dramatically the public and private issues of sexual liberation in his political novel, *Denzil Quarrier*. The result, however, had been less than successful, the conflict between public and private morality being presented through a series of unlikely melodramatic contrivances. Lilian, the heroine, is in the end seen to be no more than a passive and pitiable victim of liberal ideals and malignant personal forces. In *The Odd Women*, by contrast, the feminists themselves are the promoters and defenders of liberal ideas, and the representative bearers of the inevitable conflict between ideal and existence.

The profound influence here is undoubtedly Henry James's *The Bostonians*, which appeared five years earlier. There is no direct evidence that Gissing had read James's novel of transcendental feminism; however, the parallels and similarities between the two works are too extensive to be accidental. The tense relationship between Olive Chancellor and Verena Tarrant in James's novel, with its suggestions of lesbian affection and jealousy on the part of the older woman, is repeated in the partnership of Gissing's Mary Barfoot and Rhoda Nunn. The tension is heightened in both novels by the appearance of a distant male cousin of the older feminist. Both heroes are presented as hedonists, their 'easy' natures contrasted with the energy and intensity of their militant cousins. They each set out, initially as a game, to 'rescue' the younger partner from theories and cant about freedom. The development of the plot is also similar in both works, for the unfavourable light in which the older feminist presents the hero to her younger companion – Mary Barfoot, for instance, portrays her cousin Everard as a callous seducer – becomes the basis of the later protractions, misunderstandings and conflicts of the rescue. There is in *The Odd Women* a significant reversal in the attitudes of the two women. For here it is the older Mary Barfoot who is more pliant and sympathetic to the 'natural' impulses of women, and the younger Rhoda Nunn who preaches a doctrine of asceticism and militant celibacy. This is worth examining, for it has significant bearing on our understanding of the typicality and historical accuracy of both works.

John Goode, for instance, has distinguished the portrayal of historical reality in *The Bostonians* from the limiting perspective of the controlling centre of consciousness in James's later novels where characters are put increasingly between the reader and the situation.[14] In *The Bostonians*, he argues, individual consciousness is not absolved from the social world presented; rather, it illuminates the greater social theme. Characters are in this sense *representative* figures. Indeed this is the basis of the inclusiveness and progressive nature of James's work which has 'nothing to do with political attitudes' but 'with the attempt to create something that competes with reality through a pretension to objectivity and saliency'.[15] Reality in other words is not presented as a sensitive awareness of social life 'that really forms a donnee'; rather, the novel's claim to historical accuracy lies, in specifically Lukácsian terms, in its representation of typical characters in typical situations which display the interaction of the general and the particular.

Gissing's novel cannot be said to suffer by comparison. Though Gissing's 'odd' or 'superfluous' women would seem to be untypical in their marginality and exclusion, the basis of characterisation is not individual psychology separate from historical and social forces, or a given social milieu. The condition of 'oddness', like that of exile in *New Grub Street* and *Born in Exile*, involves desire for integration and refusal of the terms of incorporation, forming a conflictual nexus of the general and the particular, of social forces and individual lives. But more than this, Gissing concretises through personal interrelationships conflicting ideological tendencies at work in society. In the opposing characters of Mary Barfoot and Rhoda Nunn, for instance, Gissing gives an account of historical developments and conflicts within the feminist movement that is arguably more accurate than James's satirical portrayal of feminist types, and in the end more progressive in its refusal of a consolatory appeal to sympathy and experience over the possibilities of historical change. The consequence, as we shall see in examining the novel, is a dilemma that has always given trouble to a critical tradition based predominantly on ideas of sympathy and imaginative identification.

One of the two feminist leaders in the novel, Mary Barfoot clearly represents a more modest approach to social change. Her address on 'Woman as an Invader' may display a strenuous opposition to Ruskin's idealised view of women, but her programme of reform is far more modest than her revolutionary rhetoric would suggest:

'I want to do away with that common confusion of the words womanly and womanish, and I see very clearly that this can only be effected by an armed movement, an invasion by women of the spheres which men have always forbidden us to enter.' (XIII, 135)

Mary Barfoot's energies are directed towards helping the 'surplus' women who have not married. Her acceptance of marriage as the natural sphere for women would seem seriously to weaken her appeal for a radical transformation of woman's social status. Her odd women must inevitably remain odd. Indeed her demand for female education is at once reactionary and utilitarian. The promotion of an educated womanhood, she argues, will prove beneficial to husbands and useful to society. It will eradicate woman's 'paltriness' which has 'proved a curse to men', and produce a labour force suited to carry out administrative tasks in an increasingly organised society.

This acceptance of the existing social order is reinforced by a further limitation of her notion of the odd women to the 'daughters of educated people', to those whose very gentility has left them ill-equipped to succeed or even survive in a competitive society. It is a restriction which provokes one character in the novel to upbraid her for limiting her humanity 'by the artificial divisions of society' (IV). In fact Mary Barfoot's conservative reformism provides an important example of the actual mechanism of effective social change. The historical significance of this is to some extent obscured by the ideological synchronies of the narrative, for the very narrowness of her aims and activities belongs more accurately with the early phase of feminist activism in the 1860s and 1870s, rather than with the period of the late 1880s in which the novel is set. The appeal for the self-dependence of surplus women, for instance, paraphrases certain influential proposals made by Harriet Martineau as far back as 1859.[16] Moreover the idea that the problem of these 'odd' or 'redundant' women was mainly to be found among the upper and educated sections of society is also characteristic of the earlier phase of feminist argument.[17] Indeed Jessie Boucherett, the founder in the 1860s of the Society for Promoting the Employment of Woman, has been identified as the probable life model for Mary Barfoot.[18] One may want to quarrel with the relevance of such literal correspondence, but the effort of Jessie Boucherett and Mary Rye in training women for clerical work at Langham Place in the 1860s clearly indicates the anachronism of Gissing's portrait of the pioneering nature of Rhoda Nunn and Mary Barfoot at Great Portland Street in the 1880s.[19]

Less obviously anachronistic is Mary Barfoot's altruism. Feminism for her is a form of philanthropy directed towards work for women. It is also part of that developing view of woman's double mission as conscience of society as well as guardian of the home.[20] This extension of the ideal of woman did not seek to overthrow the traditional notions of womanhood. It encouraged the addition of 'masculine' action to what were considered to be inherently 'feminine' qualities of gentleness and sympathy:

'Of the old ideal virtues we can retain many, but we have
to add to them those which have been thought appropriate

only in men. Let a woman be gentle, but at the same time
let her be strong; let her be pure of heart, but none the
less wise and instructed.' (XIII, 136)

In giving voice to an optimism that was prominent in the
early- and mid-Victorian period of progress and expansion, Mary
Barfoot tends to emphasis the autonomy and transformative
capabilities of individual action, and to appeal to a common
'human nature' beneath the accidental inequalities of the social
order. 'I speak of human nature', she stresses in defence of
her views, 'not of the effect of institutions' (VI).

Significantly it is this tendency to separate the human and the
social which provokes disagreement from her subordinate, Rhoda
Nunn. To isolate the human in this way is for Rhoda to locate
the mainsprings of social misery within an essential, ineffaceable
human nature that cannot finally be questioned and transformed.
'Those views', she claims, 'lead only to pessimism and paralysis
of effort', to 'fishing foolish people out of the mud' (VI). She
blames the waste and inadequacy of most women's lives not
on individual women, but on the conditions of life 'as at present
arranged for them'. At the same time she spares no sympathy for
the victims of these conditions. In this she is not inconsistent,
for Rhoda's attitudes are not philanthropic. They involve a more
radical approach to social change in which 'sentimentalism' is
considered to be an encumbrance. She views her discord with
her leader not as a conflict between emotion and lack of feeling,
but between indulgent compassion and active indignation (XIII).

Rhoda would seem in effect to represent that more radical
feminism which emerged in the 1880s and 1890s out of the achieved
reforms and frank debates of the preceding decades.[21] In her
adherence to theory and rational principles, in her determination
to apply her radicalism to specific matters of everyday life, Rhoda
clearly belongs to that category of 'New Woman' who made frequent appearance in the novels of the period and became a target
of popular caricature. Gissing's characterisation would seem in
some respects to confirm the popular view. Rhoda's 'harangue'
against woman's foolishly sentimental conception of love (VI), and
her inherent distrust of men would seem to manifest that defensive
resistance to 'sexual things' which Mrs Lynn Linton attributed to
those 'born vestals of nature . . . who are unsexed by the atrophy
of their instincts'.[22] It is in these terms, for instance, that Mary

Barfoot taunts her when she seeks to act independently. 'Have you ever been in love with any man?' she asks, the redundancy of the final phrase producing something of that suggestive resonance with which Gissing succeeds in enriching his novel's contrived, somewhat schematic surface. Rhoda would also seem to confirm the popular conception of the 'modern man-haters' as recruits from 'those whose faith in one half of the human race cannot survive their own one sad experience'.[23] Her emotional development is seen to have been blighted by an unrequited adolescent passion (XIV). It is true that her early trauma is not presented in any crude sense as the origin of her later militancy, but the novel's oblique references to it would seem to suggest that it has been important in reinforcing certain latent aspects of her temperament and development, and in giving embodiment to her 'life's purpose'.

Oddness for Rhoda is no longer a statistical definition, but a posture for combat in a world of unequal and inauthentic sexual relationships. Like many of her real-life counterparts, Rhoda emphasises that it is a woman's right to choose a professional career instead of marriage. She represents that attempt on the part of the New Woman to break away from the narrow concern of the feminist movement in England with the problem of single women, and from its assumption that marriage is a woman's natural profession.[24] Masculine, intellectual, assertive: Rhoda's oddness is at once an attempt to realise a more authentic selfhood, and a defence against the reduction of the female body to the sexual imperative.

It is from this perspective that one must view Rhoda's efforts to extend her leader's limited programme of reform. Mary Barfoot's philanthropic feminism does in fact provide an important example of effective social change. The early promoters of employment for women were able to effect a significant breakdown of conventional attitudes to women. But like nineteenth-century liberalism itself, of which it was an important outgrowth, this practical altruistic feminism tended to lose its claim to radical status as the industrial process came increasingly to control and direct the political and cultural life of society. Rhoda's theoretical radicalism is an attempt to expose the inherent complicity of earlier humanitarian programmes of reform. Yet her own scientific perspective results in a posture of defiant selfhood that is unable in the end to interact with, or to effect the refusing structures of an intransigent social order.

Rhoda's appeal for asceticism is in the final analysis merely an extreme form of those 'negative attitudes towards coitus' which 'operated as patriarchal and psychological "stratagems" to limit and prohibit woman's pleasure in sexuality'.[25] Such a position is not in itself without a positive, emancipatory force.[26] A symptom of the alienating conditions it seeks to resist, woman's resistance to sexuality may also achieve a certain autonomy in refusing patriarchal claims. Yet such a 'stratagem' does not achieve genuine independence, as Rhoda's relationship with Everard Barfoot makes clear. Her austerity remains trapped within the cycle of 'dominate and be dominated' it attempts to escape; more significantly, it remains attached to a notion of female purity and predatory masculinity on which sexual hierarchy is based.

Through Rhoda, Gissing subtly presents the ideological deficiency of radical separatism, while at the same time making visible its tragic necessity on a historical plane. It is unsatisfactory and indeed mistaken in this context to interpret the novel in any simple sense as either hostile or favourable towards woman's liberation. Yet it is equally inappropriate to see Gissing's position more ambiguously as one of ironic sympathy for his admirable but not wholly attractive heroine. There is no facile idealisation of the liberating role of anti-conventional views or of woman's commitment to work, but equally there is no final accommodation of woman's claim to equality within the broad sympathies of generous masculinity.

It is interesting in this respect to compare *The Odd Women* with *The Bostonians*, where the appeal to sympathy and private selfhood over a codified response to life would seem in the end to support the hero's masculine rescue. Admittedly James's hero is viewed with irony – indeed the novel's final sentence scarcely suggests a 'happy ending'. Yet in his intended caricature of feminism, James clearly shares his hero's private vision of the need to reform the reformers, which if it does not justify a return to conventional roles becomes nevertheless a tragic rationalisation of the status quo. In *The Odd Women* Rhoda's resistance to Barfoot has an altogether different effect. Her relationship may demonstrate the inadequacy of her 'revolt against sexual instinct', but it does not invalidate her protest against the existing inequalities of sexual relations. Conventional sexuality is portrayed as a kind of game that plunges Rhoda into humiliating jealousy, and involves them both in a sordid 'struggle for domination'. It is true that Rhoda's 'intellectual predominance' is eventually eroded by Barfoot's 'show of homage', and that the effects of passion are seen to have made her conception of life 'larger, more liberal', but to the end she renounces nothing of her 'conscience' and 'sincerity'.

This disturbing vision of the compelling necessity of Rhoda's theoretical feminism is reinforced by the story of Monica Madden's marriage to the repressed Widdowson, which functions as a kind of explosive, emotional counterplot to the rational relationships of the feminists. Monica, who recognises the insufficiency of what she calls the 'old-maid factory', also furnishes the novel with an example of oppressed womanhood that would seem to authenticate Rhoda's ideal. The account of Monica's almost wilful blindness to the signs of Widdowson's neurotic obsessions about women, as she slides into the miseries of an unsuitable marriage, is both painful and intuitive. One might want to argue that the Monica–Widdowson relationship does not in fact 'challenge marriage as a norm';[27] in marrying for convenience, Monica deprives herself of the strong supporting ideology of romantic love which has been seen to sustain the marriage choice in the 'isolated' conditions of modern family life.[28] Yet it is clear that their marriage is meant to interrogate the conditions of repression that produce the harmonious norm.

The Monica–Widdowson relationship also makes visible the hideous basis of the chivalric 'rescue'. In saving Monica from the moral dangers of her life as a shop-girl, Widdowson displays an unstable mixture of sentimental gallantry and deep sexual dread. He is also motivated by a desire for the kind of authority he lacks in ordinary life. A clerk all his days 'like so many thousands of men', Widdowson suffers the 'frantic misery' of a man unable to live up to society's idea of masculinity. He imagines marriage in Ruskinian terms as a sacred haven in a hostile and wicked world.

The subsequent collapse of Widdowson's dream is the result of Monica's self-protective gestures of independence. Monica's rebellion submits to the compulsions of a rootless, cultureless society, and gives support, in the view of one critic of Gissing's 'liberationist' novels, 'to the conventional, and wholly reactionary case for women's subordination and return to "maternity" and the protections of conjugal life'.[29] In fact the terms of Gissing's reproach is much more ambiguous. Though Monica's death in childbirth may be a somewhat glib and unsatisfactory way of resolving the problems raised in the novel, it does not suggest the

kind of nemesis and melodramatic progress one associates with
the wayward wife of Victorian fiction. The patterns of irony are
here more finely balanced. If Widdowson is a sexual tyrant, his
tyranny is nevertheless located in the social and psychological
oppressions of a society which compels men to exact their
own submissions within the intimacy of sexual relationships.
Likewise Monica may be presented as an unreflecting follow-
er of 'nature's bidding' in a world where nature has become
synonymous with rampant individualism, but she also represents
a genuine opposition to the 'old-fashioned' ideal of marriage,
whose coercions are all on show. Unlike Gissing's short serial
novel *Eve's Ransom*, in which the failure of the rescue would
seem to support a furtive reversion to the old ideal, *The Odd
Women* renounces any such stratagem of consolatory resolution.

This refusal is also evident in the Rhoda–Barfoot sequence
which would seem to favour the final pragmatism of Barfoot's
conventional marriage. It is Rhoda's ideal of independence after
all which in the end stands denuded. Yet through Gissing
may expose the inadequacies of feminist resistance, there is
no final appeal in the novel for a return to sexual hierarchy.
Rather, the projected image is of Rhoda's continuing rejection
of the sexual imperative and the terms of incorporation which,
however negative in itself, nevertheless marks her unremitting
attempt to enter history, rather than renounce it by accepting
the terms of a traditional patriarchal resolution.

The novel ends on a poignantly ambiguous note as Rhoda
nurses the child of the dead Monica during a visit to the sole
survivor of the pathetically child-like Madden sisters:

> Rhoda, still nursing, sat down on a garden bench. She gazed
> intently at those diminutive features. . . . The dark, bright
> eye was Monica's. As the baby sank into sleep, Rhoda's
> vision grew dim; a sigh made her lips quiver, and once
> more she murmured, 'Poor little child!'   (XXI, 336)

Though Rhoda may claim that the cause flourishes 'like the green
bay tree', the very situation of the child indicates the limits of
feminist reform, and the difficulty of uniting theory and practice.
The child's likeness to her mother forbodes a cyclical repetition.
'Make a brave woman of her', Rhoda urges; but Alice Madden's
dreamy talk of opening a school recalls the impracticality that

has been responsible for the family's disintegration. If the novel here undercuts Rhoda's optimism, however, it does so not in order to urge 'the establishment of a true mutuality', nor indeed to display anything so comforting as a balance 'between sadness, and a genuine springing optimism'.[30] Rather, the scene indicates both the necessity and the ineffectualness of Rhoda's oddness and self-exclusion in a world of feeble womanhood, in a final image of fearful, tragic impassibility.

7

Towards the Vortex

*The brilliant refinement spins down to extinction
. . . London is the great dying place.*

H. G. Wells

H. G. Wells, in a sympathetic and critically discerning article
of 1897, welcomed what he saw to be a 'steady elimination' of the
'exponent character' from Gissing's novels, and a 'fading with
their progress' of the quality of bias towards 'the hopeless ideal
of scholarly refinement'.[1] This partiality had, in Wells's view,
diminished the reality and truthfulness of Gissing's earlier work.
In *The Whirlpool*, which appeared that year, Wells discovered a
distinct turning away from 'the insufficiency of the cultivated
life and its necessary insincerities' to 'the vivid appreciation
of things as they are'.[2] Gissing promptly corrected his friend's
misinterpretation of his hero's enthusiasm for athleticism and
Empire, claiming that 'in all he says, he is simply expressing
his hopeless recognition of facts which fill him with disgust':

> Thus and thus – says he – is the world going; no refusing
> to see it; it stares us in the eye; but what a course for it
> to take! – He talks with a little throwing-up of the arm,
> and in a voice of quiet sarcasm.[3]

It is a mood of sardonic resignation which Gissing identifies as
his 'own habit of mind of late years':

> I have come to recognise a course of things which formerly
> I could not – or would not – perceive; and I do it with just
> that tossing of the head – involuntary, of course. I believe that

127

all I love and believe in is going to the devil; at the same time I try to watch with interest this procession of destruction.[4]

Gissing clearly aims to correct Wells's misunderstanding of his work, but his claims to satirical detachment confirm rather than refute the distinct change of tone and structure which Wells identifies as 'a progress' and 'emancipation from the idealising stress'. It is not that Gissing renounces his former attachment to spacious culture; nor is it simply that his heroes no longer triumph – this has been true since *New Grub Street* which on one level measures 'the impracticality of the refined ideal'.[5] Rather, that shift lies in the evident inability of the favoured hero to stand for an alternative attitude or ideal that could resist the process of destruction and self-assertion in society as a whole.

This is reflected in several ways in the two major novels of Gissing's final years – *In the Year of Jubilee* and *The Whirlpool*. The city experience which they describe has altered. The structural conception of the novels continues to be Gissing's characteristic 'grouping of characters and incidents . . . about some social influence or some far-reaching movement of humanity',[6] but the situation of the characters is no longer that conflict between desire for autonomy and need for integration that one finds in the literary hacks of *New Grub Street*, or of the liberationists of *The Odd Women*. The focus here is on the excitements and extravagances of those more leisured, suburban groups created by new markets and the profits of Empire. The dominant note of these works remains one of cultural protest. Gissing's recollections of the Jubilee celebrations, and Carlylean image of 'the whirlpool', function as controlling metaphors of the pervasive influence of capitalism and Empire; they serve to convey the authorial note of irony and scorn. yet the very absence of an alternative ideal or way of life that might resist these vortical influences serves to deprive the reader of any final privileged perspective for resolving the conflicts explored. In this new world of expanding consciousness and freedom, the tragic focus is no longer the hero, torn between humane values and a refusing society; it becomes the heroine, who even in the midst of her suburban freedoms is compelled to submit to the traditional sanctions of sexual and social oppression.

There has been a strong tendency to see these novels, together with *The Odd Women*, as purely illustrative 'studies in vulgarism'.[7] It is true that in these novels female desire is seen with pessimism and repugnance to submit to the dehumanising forces of the new urbanised society emerging amid the ruins of the old world. Yet although Gissing can be seen to enact a kind of masculine vengeance upon his wayward, unconventional heroines, it is clear that his work is not intended simply as an admonition to rebellious and independent womanhood. His tone of moral reproach co-exists with a deepening sense of impasse and unequivocal submission to inevitable struggle and 'life as it is'. Blame in this climate of perplexing fatalism shifts away from individuals to the total social system which encourages surrender to spontaneous, unreflecting life.

However, it is precisely the nature of this compassionate acquittal that has most exasperated critics. For the acceptance of struggle as the inescapable law of life would seem a dishonest and finally hypocritical way to support 'the necessary subordination of women to men', in pointing defeated womanhood back to the protections of marriage and the home.[8] Yet this unfavourable critical view of Gissing's 'liberationist' novels finds its rebuttal in Gissing's own refusal of conjugal life as a refuge and sanctuary from the contentions of society. There is no going back in these novels to the comforts and consolations of the past. That is not to say that Gissing recognises the legitimacy of woman's drive towards social identity outside marriage, or in any sense endorses the new spirit and vitality of the age. His tone, though now more generous, remains sardonic. The conflict between his abhorrence of the new and his acceptance of the inevitability of self-assertion emerges in these novels in a double-vision. Here, as we shall see, it is woman who is the tragic centre of the action, both debased by her absorption in the world of commodities and false stimulations, yet by the same token resisting the debasement and curb man would impose on her in order to reassure his own masculinity and sexual power. Bearers of aspiration, symbols of dissolution: the heroines of these significant portrayals of life in the 1890s look with a radical, finally tragic longing beyond the inadequacies of the past and degradations of the present to the possibilities of a world whose nature cannot yet be guessed.

I THE 'WORTHY' SEDUCER: *IN THE YEAR OF JUBILEE*

In the Year of Jubilee was published by Lawrence and Bullen in three volumes in December 1894. It was the last of Gissing's novels to appear in the traditional three-decker form, which was effectively abandoned by publishers in that year. Although far from successful from a commercial point of view, *In the Year of Jubilee* was recognised from the first as a significant exploration of new attitudes to marriage and woman's role in society. The idea for a new book, to be called 'A Girl's Wild Oats', had come to Gissing on the day he abandoned his novel of provincial life, *The Iron Gods*, within twenty pages of its completion.[9] Entitled 'Miss Lord of Camberwell' until its revision in proof, the story centres on the heroine's choice between the plebeian advertising agent, Luckworth Crewe, and the socially superior Lionel Tarrant who eventually seduces her. By an elaborate plot complication characteristic of the Victorian three-decker, the heroine is forced into concealing her marriage and subsequent pregnancy by the death of her father, since she cannot benefit by his will if she marries before the age of twenty-six. Abandoned by her husband, Nancy is seen to develop from girlish wantonness to patient heroism, first as a single parent, and finally as a reconciled wife, accepting the terms of Tarrant's 'bachelor' marriage. Gissing's evocation of the euphoric mood of Queen Victoria's Diamond Jubilee celebrations of 1887 provides the novel with a meaningful social context. The Dickensian profusion of character and sub-plot surrounding the seduction elaborates and repeats Gissing's directing vision of 'the extending and deepening Vulgarity' and 'blackguardism . . . pouring forth over the society'.[10]

In the Year of Jubilee presents, in its account of lower middle-class life in Camberwell, an ironic portrait of one corner – the consumer end – of the 'vast inhuman metropolis'. The viciousness and spurious gentility of the Peachey household; the hysteric emphasis of the Morgan family on educational success; the vulgarity of the advertising agent, Luckworth Crewe, unrolling the future in his 'coloured picture of Whitsand pier': through a series of pen portraits, Gissing constructs a vision of complete cultural collapse that has a close thematic relationship with *The Nether World* and *New Grub Street*. The difference here is that the 'wages of sin' in the context of the 'world of satisfactions' opened up by relative prosperity, are depicted not in the bleakly pessimistic tones of the earlier novels, but with a savage comedy that prefigures to some extent Waugh's satires of cultural decadence and fatuity over thirty years later. The very grossness of such characters as the shadowy Mrs Damerel, with her fraudulent refinements, and the philistine 'suburban deity', Samuel Barmby, educated 'by dint of busy perusal of penny popularities', gives a ludic edge to Gissing's criticism. This suggestion of comedy is reinforced by certain cyclic patterns in the narrative. There is something finally grotesque, for instance, in Arthur Peachey's ignominious return to marital 'martyrdom' and another child, and in Jessica Morgan's reappearance at the close of the novel with 'her crazy malice grotesquely disguised' in the uniform and 'hideous bonnet' of the Salvation Army. There is a suggestion, as in all satire, not only of mockery, but also of a kind of self-mockery that would seem to derive from a bitter acceptance of the futility of all protest.

In the Year of Jubilee is pervaded by Gissing's deepening sense of the bewildering extensions and expansions of city life. Gissing, as Raymond Williams has argued, belongs with those nineteenth- and twentieth-century urban writers for whom the city is no longer simply a 'generalized social scene', but the very 'form of modern life' itself.[11] The country in Gissing's novels is no longer the domain of alternative organic values. It is a place of temporary leisure and holiday, connected to, and indeed part of the extended network of urban life. The city is of course the setting of all that Gissing most dreads and despises – struggle, misery, loss of connection. But for Gissing as for other writers of the 'urban revolution', it is also the site of his own freedom as an artist. His particular response remains in this respect on the side of isolation and lonely watchfulness.[12] One finds in his work little of that pleasure in the freedom and vitality of the city, in what Baudelaire identified as the aesthetic possibilities afforded the fertile artist in merging himself with the crowd. His laughter at the oddness and absurdities of city life, for instance, is never 'self-forgetful'.[13] It remains, in H. G. Wells's view, 'entirely enclosed in a defensive and conscious "scorn" for the "baser" orders and "ignoble" types'.[14] Sharp, detached, caustic: Gissing's style sets the terms of this divorce between observer and observed. And yet, if the terms of that response are finally negative, the response of 'the lonely observer set over against the generalised mass',[15] there is in *In the Year of Jubilee*, at least, a new awareness of the excitements and exhilaration that the rush and welter of city life can produce. The characters in the novel are not those alienated 'unclassed' individuals that one finds in Gissing's earlier works, compelled to an undignified struggle for subsistence. Here Gissing portrays a relatively affluent, increasingly variegated suburban middle

class, avid for culture, comfort and gentility. The image of
the city changes. It is no longer a place of mean, gloomy
streets and districts where men work and sleep. Rather, it is a
world of traffic, city crowds and advertisement signs seen from
a moving tramcar or from the top of a monument. The images of
oppression and uniformity remain in the descriptions of the new
streets of suburban Camberwell 'built to one pattern by the mile',
but the tone is one of 'genuinely ambiguous irony'[16] that responds
to the cleanness and 'breadth' of suburbia, and the proximity
of open fields. Grove Lane, for instance, is seen to have

> a certain picturesqueness, enhanced by the growth of fine
> trees on either side. . . . There are small cottages overgrown
> with creepers, relics of Camberwell's rusticity; rows of tall
> and of squat buildings that lie behind grassy plots, railed
> from the road; larger houses that stand in their own gardens,
> hidden by walls. Narrow passages connect the Lane with its
> more formal neighbour Camberwell Grove; on the other side
> are ways leading to Denmark Hill, quiet, leafy. From the top
> of the Lane, where Champion Hill enjoys an aristocratic
> seclusion, is obtainable a glimpse of open fields and of a
> wooded horizon southward. (I.iii, 13)

It is this perceived margin of freedom in the novel that
would seem to allow the possibility of a measure of happiness
and repose in the fate of the heroine. Nancy Lord's development
from youthful romanticism and wilfulness to the maturities of her
difficult and unconventional marriage becomes, as Gillian Tindall
has suggested, 'the classic theme of an individual finding himself
or herself through tribulation'.[17] Nancy is not of course exempted
form the novel's cynical critique of the vulgarism and wanton
spirit of the times. It is after all the effects of her 'sham' culture
and education which are held up for ironic inspection. Robert
Selig has commented in this context on Gissing's opposition
to those educators of girls who were 'allies of the scientists':
it is seen as an indication of their spiritual and intellectual
deficiency that 'Nancy Lord studies evolution, Fanny French
inorganic chemistry and botany, and Jessica Morgan reviews
"Geographical Progression".'[18] Gissing's prescriptions are here
nakedly Arnoldian. The novel, with an inverted religiosity similar
to modern agnostic distaste for the application of consumer

techniques to religion, reflects ironically on Nancy's failure to perceive the incongruity of a scriptural tract 'inserted between the Soap and the Jam' (I.viii). In the description of the Jubilee celebrations there is a note of contempt at the spectacle of Nancy's submission to the hilarity and 'stupid contentment' of the crowd:

> Nancy forgot her identity, lost sight of herself as an individual. . . . She did not think, and her emotions differed little from those of any shop-girl let loose. The 'culture', to which she laid claim, evanesced in this atmosphere of exhalations.   (I.vii, 68–9)

The mood of recklessness is reawakened amidst the vulgarities of Teignmouth promenade, with its 'loungers' and its opportunities for self-display. Gissing describes the stirrings of Nancy's 'physical attraction' to Tarrant with a frankness that challenges the traditional reticences of the Victorian novel:

> A debilitating climate and absolute indolence favoured that impulse of lawless imagination which had first possessed her on the evening of Jubilee Day. With luxurious heedlessness she cast aside every thought that might have sobered her; even as she at length cast off all her garments, and lay in the warm midnight naked upon her bed.   (II.iv, 113)

On the face of it, the image of Nancy's wantonness conveys a genuine horror. Yet its very explicitness would seem to betray a hidden fascination with the liberating possibilities of woman's active sexuality.

It is an ambivalence which pervades the novel's whole treatment of the conventional motif of seduction and the 'fallen woman'. In the mid-Victorian novel, as Françoise Basch has pointed out, 'female frivolity, the puerile aspiration to become a lady, are still seen as the principle causes of the fall'.[19] This serves to some extent to extenuate the 'fallen' heroine, allowing a criticism of society's double standard, and implicitly of 'aristocratic' values. The downfall of the lowly heroine – of Hetty Sorrel, for example, in George Eliot's *Adam Bede* – is seen to be caused not only by sexual instinct, but by circumstances which have made her the victim of male sexuality. Yet this extenuation is based on the notion of woman's asexual nature that paradoxically reinforces the double standard it would claim to challenge. Woman continues to be seen as the spiritual custodian of man's inherently carnal appetites. *In the Year of Jubilee* clearly suspends and questions certain aspects of the motif it puts to work. Though Nancy is shown to succumb to the charms of Tarrant's 'cultured' voice and air of breeding, Tarrant's aristocratic pretensions are punctured by her own clumsy reference to his family's commercial links. Her fate likewise displays little of that disproportionate punishment which becomes in *Adam Bede* 'a realistic perception of the working of a double standard'.[20] Rather, as Adrian Poole has suggested, the narrative 'deliberately goes *beyond* the supposedly crucial cataclysm of the heroine's sexual "fall"'.[21] It is a movement that produces a questioning of received notions of class, culture and sexual hierarchy, establishing an image of the heroine's engaging independence of obstructive social and sexual conventions. And yet it must be said that the providential solution of Nancy's marriage to her seducer indicates the narrative's continuing adherence to those traditional values that are brought into question. The result is a series of 'silences' at the centre of the novel. It is this which makes *In the Year of Jubilee* so exasperating. The voice of protest and freedom for oppressed womanhood is never completely silenced, but it can only be heard athwart the novel's own declarations, with their shoring up of the traditional claims of authority, patriarchy and class.

In the account of the seduction, for instance, Nancy is criticised for surrendering to the 'lure of crude imagination'; yet the voice which lures her is the voice which mocks with ironic gratification her unreflecting accord with the spirit of her time 'advertisements and all' (II.iv). Tarrant is seen to exploit the very servitude to images against which he protests. Indeed his avowed aestheticism begins to look shabbily opportunistic in comparison with Nancy's spontaneous, if immature 'self-abandonment'. The problem here is not so much that Tarrant is 'never really placed',[22] but that the authorial perspective would seem actually to support Tarrant's claim to social and moral authority. Tarrant's appeal to Keats's Teignmouth may be finally bland and insubstantial, but it is all of a piece with the author's own encomium to the unspoiled world of pastoral tranquillity lying inland from the boarding houses and 'smoking traffic' of the modern resort (II.iv). Blame is shifted away from the suave, predatory hero to the 'uncultured' heroine. In response to Nancy's affected interest in Helmholtz, Tarrant recites with genuine emotion some verses of Keats. There is an implicit irony in having him select 'La belle dame sans merci'. But whereas the poem itself can be seen to provide an ironic perspective on both the insufficiency of the real and the folly of the Knight's pursuit of the inhuman, the ballad would seem to be invoked in the novel merely as an ironic comment on the delusive seducements of the prosaic world.

Tarrant's position is in fact subjected to a belated scrutiny following his hasty marriage. The chambers of Staple Inn, his financial insecurity, the facetious modernity of the 'Hodiernals': the whole tone of this biographical recapitulation would seem to be at one with the novel's satirical exposure of contemporary life. In blaming his folly on his 'habitual idleness, and the vagueness of his principles', Tarrant himself would seem to recognise the inadequacy of his specious medievalism and 'dainty enjoyment of his own limitless leisure', though he excuses himself with the thought that he has only followed the impulses of nature. If the seduction has been marked by 'unanticipated impulses . . . quite inconsistent with heartless scheming', then Nancy's 'self-surrender' has been likewise free of 'coarseness' or 'artful fencing'. Yet love excuses Nancy's 'self-abandonment' only 'to a certain point'. Tarrant, with the characteristic exculpation of the defendant in a trial of rape, comes to the conclusion that Nancy's 'beauty . . . had lured him on'. In seeking to explain her failure to exercise 'the common prudence of womanhood', he is driven finally to blame 'the circumstance of her origin and training . . . she illustrated the social peril, the outcome of modern follies. . . . A result of charlatan "education" operating upon crude character' (III.ii). It is true that the whole scene is a dramatic rendering of Tarrant's confused state of mind, but the very sensitivity of the novel's psychological analysis gives an unexpected centrality to Tarrant's point of view. Indeed the final basis of his self-extenuation – that Nancy lacks hereditary refinement and educated culture – is precisely the focus of the novel's own ironic account of her abandonment to the 'spirit of her time'.

The hasty marriage ceremony and the factitiousness of the legacy plot would seem merely to gloss the obvious fact that in practice Nancy's situation 'is exactly like that of an unmarried mother'.[23] Yet the stipulation of the will which makes it necessary for them to conceal the marriage serves paradoxically to place Tarrant in an unfavourable light. It is not only that Tarrant is callous and egotistical in abandoning Nancy to a

life of loneliness and duplicity, but that he seems positively
blind to his own disingenuousness in pleading for concealment
and the morality of 'separate lives'. With his desertion the
narrative shifts to Nancy's heroic search for a moral alternative
to 'coarse vitality' and 'shame' culture. Her desire for 'some
honest, strenuous occupation' involves a rejection of both 'mere
social excitement and the idle vanity which formerly she styled
pursuit of culture' (IV.vii). Yet her subsequent discouragement
as she walks the streets of London displays a new tension:

> In the battle of life every girl who could work a sewing-machine
> or make a match-box was of more account than she. . . . A little
> book on "employments for women", which she saw advertised
> and bought, merely heightened her discouragement. . . . She
> was a coward; she dreaded the world; she saw as never yet the
> blessedness of having money and a secure home.   (V.i, 297)

Nancy may shrink 'back into her suburban home', but she
recognises that such a withdrawal is cowardly and inadequate.

It is a tension that would seem to underlie the novel's own representation of independent womanhood. On the face of it, the novel
would seem to confirm the popular image of the 'New Woman':

> Sometimes the 'New Woman' was shown as a neurotic prey to
> hysteria and morbid self-analysis, with a constitution allegedly
> enfeebled by over-education and too much strain on the
> intellect. . . . Alternatively, the 'advanced woman' was likely
> to be credited with a hale and hearty constitution; with a
> bluff good humour likely to manifest itself in backslapping or
> the tendency to refer to intimates . . . as 'jolly good chaps'.[24]

Carol Dyehouse's account of the literary stereotypes of the 'New
Woman' refers us to the popular basis of Gissing's characterisation
of Jessica Morgan and Beatrice French. Beatrice's masculine
affectations, her fondness for colloquialisms and her virile appetite
for 'rump steak smothered in onions' and 'sound Stilton cheese'
clearly present a satirical view of the 'advanced woman' (V.iv).
Gissing might be accused in this respect of journalistic caricature.
And yet his portrait of Beatrice is also suggestive of deeper
psychological currents. Not only does the over-compensation

of her arch remarks and sly allusions betray an edge of real loneliness, but this very undercurrent of emotion and necessary affectation lends a sort of pathos and heroism to her position. Her 'independent sort of life' is seen to avoid the destructive tendencies displayed by her sisters Fanny and Ada – the former lapsing into promiscuity, the latter into shrewish violence. Indeed it is because of Beatrice that Nancy is able to win for herself a margin of self-sufficiency in fulfilling her desire 'to do something'.

Out of its conflicts, then, the novel is forced to an uneasy recognition of heroic, independent womanhood. It is precisely at this point that Tarrant is brought back from his wanderings abroad. It would seem to be an attempt on Gissing's part to reaffirm the conventions. But Tarrant's fraudulently sentimental view of Nancy and cynical urging of a double standard scarcely compel our assent:

> Faithful in the technical sense he had not been, but the casual amours of a young man caused him no self-reproach; Nancy's image remained without rival in his mind; he had continued to acknowledge her claims upon him, and, from time to time, to think of her with a lover's longing.   (V.v, 338)

Nancy's attitude of sarcasm, cold reticence and unwavering practicality, her capacity to fly 'to just those logical ineptitudes which most surely exasperate the male intelligence', would seem to expose Tarrant's male egotism and conventionality. To his plea that she free herself from dishonour and the burden of solitary struggle, Nancy's response is that she can 'see no freedom . . . I am as free as I wish to be. I have made a life for myself that satisfies me – and now you come and undo everything. I won't be tormented – I have endured enough' (V.viii). Yet there is no perspective on Tarrant's partly biological, partly Ruskinian view of woman's destiny other than Nancy herself, who is diverted by the strategic distortions and postures of marital conflict. The result is that Nancy's claim for independence can be read merely as an implicit taunt to Tarrant's male prejudices, aimed at exacting her own margin of avenging self-assertion. Furthermore the authorial rendering of Tarrant's state of mind in this scene is confined almost wholly to descriptions of his 'wonder and admiration' at Nancy's beauty, the effect of this being to forestall any real examination of his views or purpose.

I think that critics have been right to deplore this lack of editorial comment in the novel. Yet having said this, I think it is unfair to belittle Gissing's cultural critique as over-fastidious, or to 'revise' the novel in favour of Nancy's vital accord with the spirit of her time. For Gissing's conventional solution is dictated in the end not so much by a vision of woman's necessary submission to male protection, but by a pervasive, deeply fatalistic image of 'unending ineffectual toil'. Although the novel may recognise the dignity of work, work itself is identified with the degrading conditions of life in industrial society. It is a tension displayed by Nancy herself, asserting the pride she feels in earning her own living, yet moved at the same time to express her disgust at the exploitative and alienating nature of her work: 'I advise fools about the fashions, and exhibit myself as a walking fashion-plate' (V.viii). Moreover in making the 'unworthy seducer' and the 'worthy suitor' one, Gissing puts his finger on the peculiar nature of the Jubilee spirit itself. For the Jubilee celebrations

> were gigantic advertisements for the new Empire of which Victoria had come to be the crowned symbol, bringing enormous satisfaction to the masses and classes who felt that two generations of material progress were now suitably summarized in these romantic pageants.[25]

Advertisement of progress, symbol of traditional values: it is this very doubleness which makes the account of the heroine's fall seem finally so contradictory. For Gissing's whole critique of pseudo-gentility and sham culture becomes not only a contemptuous denunciation of rampant individualism, but an embarrassed recognition that traditional 'organic' categories have themselves become merely a screen for cynical exploitation and the furtherance of material and commercial ends. The world of the novel is in fact a world which, from the mid-nineteenth century, had seen a rapid 'assimilation of the English business classes to the social pattern of the gentry and aristocracy'.[26] The consequence of this, as E. J. Hobsbawn has pointed out, included 'the heavy incrustation of British public life with pseudo-medieval and other ritual, like the cult of royalty', and 'the pretence that the Englishman is a thatched cottager or a country squire at heart'.[27] Gissing's viewpoint is unmistakably meshed in this late-nineteenth-century form of romantic conservatism. Hence his attachment to Tarrant. Yet in satirising the suburban desire for refinement, Gissing paradoxically exposes the ideological necessity which perverts human aspirations to such degrading postures and simulations.

The result is a curious tension in which the novel's contradictions become the basis of its insights. Thus Nancy is seen to submit to the false stimulations of the age; yet in choosing Tarrant rather than Crewe, she is also directed by 'a contemptuous distaste for coarse vitality and vigour, whereto she had half-surrendered herself, when hopeless of the more ambitious desire' (II.iv). Her 'folly' is presented as an act of filial transgression; yet her surrender to Tarrant's 'superiority' is curiously in accord with the deepest social and cultural aspirations of her father's conservative, petty-bourgeois household. As a dealer in pianofortes to a class of people 'rabid in the pursuit of gentility', Stephen Lord is himself portrayed in the early scenes of the novel as part of that 'hire-purchase' nexus that Gissing so abhors. Yet later in the novel, Nancy is arrested by the 'tender memory' of her father as the 'guide and protector' she has foolishly disregarded (V.iv). The return here is not to an affirmation of lower-class reality itself as a kind of virtue, which Terry Eagleton has identified in the 'lower middle-class novel'.[28] Rather it is to the suburban claim to refinement that the novel itself has satirised. The result, however, is not confusion. For in so far as it is taken seriously, that 'aristocratic pretension' is to some extent 'placed'. The novel's tension is, as we have seen, most palpable in Gissing's address, which is by turns sarcastic and sensitive, contemptuously detached and sympathetically immersed in the psychology of the characters. The novel in effect seems constantly to turn in upon its own satirical generalisation in a way that confirms the maxim expressed by Gissing in *The Private Papers of Henry Ryecroft*: 'Take a man by himself and there is generally some reason to be found in him, some disposition for good.'

In the Year of Jubilee prefigures the problems of Gissing's novels in the closing years of Victoria's reign. For here the basis of Gissing's sense of autonomy and inner resistance to society becomes pitiably ineffectual in the face of the bewildering extensions and energies of modern life. Imperialism, mass culture: it is not simply that 'culture' is finally unable to oppose these developments, but that it is itself seen to submit to the very world of 'images' it claims to resist. There is in Gissing's last novels such as *The Town Traveller* and *Will Warburton* a tendency to retreat either to romance, or to sardonic laughter. *In the Year of Jubilee* keeps these tendencies in dialectical tension, exposing, in its image of the 'worthy seducer', the cultural and intellectual conditions of modern English society in its deepest, most fugitive reaches.

II   THE VANISHING CENTRE: *THE WHIRLPOOL*

The Whirlpool (1897) has with some justice been seen as a 'less extreme, more conventional' version of Flaubert's *Madame Bovary*.[29] It is a comparison that springs from the perceived resemblances in the situation of the dull, gauche, ineffectual husband and the irascible, highly strung heroine. Gissing's Alma Frothingham demonstrates the disastrous consequences of submission to the stimulations of a meretricious society, while her burning desire for pre-eminence, like Emma Bovary's sick dreams, lays bare the oppressions and stifling conventions of bourgeois domesticity. The shift here is not from traditional censure to a more compassionate view of the 'fallen woman'. The image that emerges in both novels is of a type of masculine woman – purposeful, reckless, manly, as Baudelaire wrote of Madame Bovary, in 'her ability to dream dreams'.[30]

The effect of modernity on man's inner feelings is significant in delineating Alma's neurosis and frenzied pursuit of self-fulfilment. Modernity is seen to involve an extension of remote phenomena into personal life in a way that disturbs identity and secure feelings. The importance of the newspaper as a medium of this intrusion is made visible in the account of her father's suicide. Here the very immediacy of the press report is seen to divert its readers from serious consideration of the personal and social implications of the tragedy to amused speculation about the domestic troubles of the workman who discovered the body; later in the novel, the newspapers will be shown to inflate Alma's involvement in the squalid intrigues of fashionable society into sensational public affairs, which the tabloids promise to render meaningful in a series of 'startling revelations'.

The actual correlation of this large-scale consciousness and extension of the previously remote, centres on the financial collapse of Frothingham's Loan Company. For Alma the event has a profound psychological significance, the origin of her sense of personal impotence and injury in the face of complex and uncontrollable circumstances. The collapse of the loan company also measures the limits of sympathy in a world of colossal social and economic catastrophe. Mrs Frothingham's programme of voluntary restitution may enact a spectacle of efficacious sympathy, but it exposes at the same time the limits of such sympathetic extension in a world in which human relations are based on the 'artificial' bonds of competitive struggle and financial speculation. Her 'substantial sacrifices' are in fact hedged round with suggestions of self-interest. Though the novel's hero, Harvey Rolfe, may accept her sincerity, it is significant that he should be presented as fundamentally naïve in his dealings with women (I.ix). There are indications that Mrs Frothingham desires to publish her 'benevolent sympathies' through her naïve emissary as a first step in winning her way back into society. There are also hints that she is match-making. Indeed Alma is provoked to an outburst of childish theatricality and hurt pride that will later mark the absence of honest relationship and sustaining values in society as a whole. Rolfe dispels Alma's suspicion of interference, but uncertainty about Mrs Frothingham's motives remains as part of an oblique, inferential mode of narration that mimics the confusion and complexity, the elusiveness of truth in the 'whirlpool' world of fashionable society.

I think *The Whirlpool* is more successful in this respect than *In the Year of Jubilee*. In the earlier novel, the sense of mystery and ferment surrounding Mrs Damerel and the world of the *beau monde* tends to be diffused in a series of vignettes in the margin of the work. The link between Mrs Damerel's theatricality and the advertising world of Luckworth Crewe – 'Mrs Damerel', we are told, 'looked rather like a sentimental picture in an advertisement' – is never sufficiently interrogated. Rather, such remarks tend to suggest a merely sardonic aloofness on the part of the novelist from the vulgarism of the age. In *The Whirlpool*, by contrast, the suggestions of intrigue, and even of crime, are related not only to what Raymond Williams has referred to as a new sense of "the opaque complexity of modern city life',[31] but to the perception of a new 'subjectivity' which surrenders itself to the images and stimulations of the market place. For the men and women of Gissing's metropolitan 'whirlpool', the possibility of extension lies in their very shadowiness, in their capacity to make themselves 'objects' for each other. It is this which is seen to underlie the consensus and artificiality of the coterie life-style. It is also seen to compel the silences of Sybil and Hugh Carnaby at table, talking of 'things as remote as possible from their immediate concerns'. Like Henry James in *The Awkward Age* and *What Maisie Knew*, Gissing locates the 'decadence' of the *fin de siècle* in the vanities and extravagences of a *rentier* society. Alma's role is in this respect like that of James's innocents. She registers the glittering surface of Sybil Carnaby's fashionable, metropolitan circle. The 'great gaps and voids' are there,[32] the sense of someone eavesdropping on a confused and obscure world, full of tacit intelligences; but so to is the suggestion of expanding consciousness, of what Henry James calls 'the full ironic truth'.[33] Alma's impressions register the cold narcissism beneath the charming, polished surface. And yet here there is no final appeal to the sense of knowledge that attends, say, Isabel Archer's discovery of the truth about Madame Merle in *The Portrait of a Lady*; nor does the novel confirm the reader's ironic, 'supplementary' intelligence in the manner of *What Maisie Knew*. Has Sybil committed adultery with Redgrave in order to obtain his financial help? Has the sinister Mrs Strangeways been acting as Redgrave's procuress? The 'truth' is never finally revealed, indeed is deliberately left uncertain. The effect is in the end to arrest any confident sense of completeness and coherence, or self-satisfied knowing.

This is also evident in Rolfe's response to a society grown self-indulgent on the profits of Empire. 'We're rotting at home', announces the novel's hero, 'some of us sunk in barbarism, some coddling themselves in over-refinement' (I.ii). The attitude here is one of recoil, not only from decadence, but from what he calls beating 'the big British drum'. His appeal to 'wholesome barbarism' as an antidote to over-refinement displays a trace of self-mockery in one who enjoys the culinary pleasures of the Metropolitan Club. Indeed it is Rolfe who recognises the economic basis of British imperialism and its attendant cults of militarism and of building a 'stouter race':

> 'The Empire; that's beginning to mean something. The average Englander has never grasped the fact that there was such a thing as a British Empire. He's beginning to learn it, and itches to kick somebody, to prove his Imperialism. . . . We can't make money quite so easily as we used to; scoundrels in Germany and elsewhere have dared to learn the trick of commerce. We feel sore, and it's a great relief to have our

advantages pointed out to us. By God! we are the British Empire,
and we'll just shown 'em what *that* means!' (III.xiii, 450)

Imperialism has emerged, as Rolfe recognises, not so much
from a collective sense of moral superiority and national achievement, but from a consciousness of waning power in the face
of colonial competition. The sense of national stagnation and
decline, of 'rotting at home', is here placed in a wider context
in which athleticism cannot finally be seen as a 'wholesome'
opposition to decadence. It is not only that the ideal of the
'conquering, civilising Briton' is seen in the end to support
the sordid materialism of 'the buccaneering shopkeeper, the
whiskey-distiller with a rifle', but that both imperialism and
decadence manifest the same desire to escape from a colourless,
conventional existence – one in heroic, impetuous adventure; the
other in a precious, *carpe diem* aestheticism. Both are rooted in
the effect in the same Social Darwinian ideology – one endorsing
the struggle between nations and individuals; the other urging
the evolutionary claims of irrational instinct and 'infinite forms
of life'. Thus Redgrave, the 'polished capitalist' who expounds
a Paterian ideal of 'experience' as a means of escaping the
philosophies of a stereotype world, is not only able to sympathise
with the conquering Briton, but actually identifies his own
desire to 'live in imagination' as having 'something of the same
spirit' (II.ix). Gissing grasps the distinctive character of an age
which produced both a Rudyard Kipling and an Oscar Wilde.

Yet though Rolfe is not to be identified with the chauvinism of
Empire, his ironic retreat behind its rhetoric, taken together with
his confessed state of 'perpetual scepticism' and 'profound igno-
rance of everything', indicates his lack of access to an alternative
ideology capable of counteracting the universal sense of decline.
His correction is seen to be neutralised by his fatalism. 'Circumstance', we are told, 'was Harvey's god' (I.iii). In marrying Alma,
Rolfe may desire to redeem her from the 'vulgarism' of fashionable
society; but paradoxically it is Alma who is the true Utopian,
'whether yearning for public triumphs, or eager to lead a revolution in domestic life' (I.xii). In *The Whirlpool* there is nothing of
that exasperating withdrawal of ironic perspective from the hero
that one finds in *In the Year of Jubilee*. It is not only that the heroine
is here more articulate and incisive in challenging male assumptions: 'You think that you know the world, whilst I am ignorant of

it, and that it's a sort of duty to offer warnings' (I.x). Rather, the ironic force lies in the novel's own exposure of the insufficiency of the offered alternatives – rural simplicity in Wales; suburban freedom in Pinner; the commitment to technological progress – as a means of escaping the debasements of metropolitan life.

In the face of this vanishing moral centre, Alma's death has more than a merely illustrative force. Her 'progress' does in fact expose important features of contemporary moral and cultural failure – notably the idolatrous delusions of a pseudo-Bohemian life-style, and the manoeuvring of the creative artist into a new role as either pander to public taste or idol of the coterie – but it does so in a way that avoids the suggestion of schematic and melodramatic convenience such as mars Gissing's earlier novel, *Denzil Quarrier*, in which the heroine's suicide supports a conservative resolution. There is in effect no support for Rolfe's condemnation of professional life 'for a married woman', nor for Alma's own painful resolve to 'be a good woman, rule her little house, bring up her child, and have no will but her husband's' (III.ix). Indeed Alma's acceptance of 'circumstance' and 'hereditary shame' is represented not as an ascent to wisdom, but as a repressive purgatorial resolve which is attended by a symptomatic recurrence of insomnia and drug dependence. In her final days of exile, nursing her 'baffled ambition' in 'a small house in Gunnersby', Alma remains tragically divided between the desire for self-validation in a world she knows to be merely 'whirl and glare', and a life of 'house-ruling' which submits to the intolerable conditions of feminine sacrifice and restraint. The work stands in the end not as a register of a new knowledge and transformation, but rather of the scepticism and impotence of the bewildered spectator. Yet though Gissing's position within ideology may prevent him from revising his fictional method in a way that might satisfy the demand for moral and epistemological certainty, it is this very incapacity to reassure the reader which constitutes the effectiveness of his work. Indeed it is in this context that *The Whirlpool* stands as Gissing's last major novel. For here in the conflicts of female ambition and conjugal oppression, the moral imperatives of traditional institutions and personal validation clash in a way that resists the gratifications of ironic knowing, or traditional moral resolves. It was with prophetic satisfaction as well as regret that Gissing wrote of the novel: 'It is doubtful if I shall do anything better, or anything again so good.'[34]

Conclusion

'He stands for something', Arnold Bennett wrote of Gissing in 1889. 'His words have authority, and his name carries respect even among "my ordinary readers" which will not buy him.'[1] The reputation that Gissing enjoyed in the last years of his life is in part to be attributed to a kind of veneration and respectability that sometimes comes to grace the survivor of an older generation of writers. Gissing's name was linked increasingly in the late 1890s with those of Meredith and Hardy. Yet his high standing is also to be related to a growing note of tolerance and resignation in his fiction. It was a change that delighted critics and reviewers who had been accusing Gissing since the early 1880s of an exaggerated, dreary realism. 'The later books seemed to open possibilities of brilliant promise', commented one critic shortly after Gissing's death. 'The bitterness had become softened, the general protest against the sorry scheme of human things seemed to be passing into a kind of pity for all that suffers, and an acceptance with thankfulness of life's little pleasures.'[2]

This favourable view of the later novels has never been shared by subsequent readers. James Joyce, coming upon *The Crown of Life* three years after Gissing's death, responded scornfully to its passages of inflated pastoralism and commonplace idealisation of love.[3] Joyce himself was clearly inhibited from recognising the peculiar merits of Gissing's work. It is not only that he appears to be unacquainted with Gissing's most successful studies of English lower middle-class life. His response seems also to have been largely determined by a modernist rejection of old-fashioned ways of writing. Yet Joyce incisively identifies the spuriousness of romance – its lack of genuine reality or bearing – in the work of a writer whose critical perspective remains essentially urban.

Gissing's retreat to nature, or to that 'dogged disillusioned affirmation of the quotidian' which Eagleton has identified in the work of Bennett and Wells,[4] can in part be accounted for in terms of Gissing's professional response to the changing conditions of publication and marketing after 1894, the year which saw the final termination of the three-decker system of publication.[5] In Gissing's short, more obliquely narrated fictions after that year, we encounter the familiar themes and motifs of his work turned to ironic effect in support of the aesthetic satisfaction of 'knowing'. The real significance of that retreat, however, is to be located in the weakening of Gissing's traditional intellectual radicalism in a world of restless expansion and enlarging inner worlds. One finds Gissing increasingly estranged from English society in these last years as he spent more and more time abroad. In accounts of his life, the tendency has been to present this period as one of autumnal peace and relative prosperity, in which Gissing at last found a congenial woman companion in Gabrielle Fleury. But the final impression one gets from his diary and correspondence is of a life of restless wanderings, homesickness and lonely exile. His most popular work of these last years, *The Private Papers of Henry Ryecroft*, is dominated by a note of chronic melancholy and nostalgic longing for English food and English virtues. Ryecroft, the fictional diarist, is represented as writing in rural retirement in Exeter, but the contrast between foreign lands and his recollections of his 'dear island' (Summer, II) suggests his physical as well as spiritual exile from an England which Gissing admitted to be 'much more an aspiration than a memory'.[6]

The inherent weakness of Gissing's traditional attachments; his inability to live at peace with his society, or to find a new basis for relationship in cosmopolitan life through which to express the terms of his separateness: these have particularly disabling consequences in *The Crown of Life*. Piers Otway's vision of the City indicates a world where the forces of oppression have become obscure, but systematic. He sees the triumphant façade of its 'huge rampart-streets' as part of a huge machine which reduces man to 'a portion of an inconceivably complicated mechanism' (XX). The novel itself opposes militarism, newspaper jingoism and 'hard selfishness'. Lee Hannaford, the inventor of new explosives; Arnold Jacks, 'a high-bred bull dog' whose religion of Empire amounts to 'looking after his own and other people's dividends': these characters conflate civilisation with racial superiority in a commonplace justification of imperialism, but are themselves seen to be unresponsive to true culture and civilising influences. Jack's soulless pursuit of dividends is continued into his private life in a practical and passionless acquisition of a wife to 'civilize the drawing room'. Similarly, Hannaford's dreams of carnage unite with a 'puritanical coldness' towards his wife. Their sterility is seen to be a symptom of a new, acquisitive, power-hungry society which channels and perverts the vital sources of man's instinctual physical life. The correlation of barren sexuality with a wider pattern of social and cultural disintegration becomes a significant index of the interpenetration of the private and the social, of inner and outer worlds.

It is a projection that points forward to one of the central preoccupations of D. H. Lawrence's work. Here, as in Lawrence, hostility to the atomisation of modern, urban industrial society becomes a rejection of the forms of sterile relationship that such a society creates. At the root of Lawrence's critique of 'mechanical' principles is an ideal of an organic, pre-industrial social order that he inherits from the nineteenth-century social critics. But within this perspective, Lawrence has access to alternative, essentially working-class values through which he is able to interrogate and effectively expose the violence of oppression at work in society as a whole. Gissing's indebtedness to the same Romantic humanist heritage is characterised, by contrast, by the significant degree to which he shares the traditional values and assumptions of his society. There is in Gissing's novels nothing of that deep sense of instinctual life that one finds in Lawrence; nothing of that discovery made by Joyce and the modernist urban writers of 'language itself' as 'the most deeply known human community'.[7] It is this absence of alternative values which compels Gissing in *The Crown of Life* to an eccentric, rather desperate appeal to 'Slavophilism' as a remedy to British imperialism. It is a literary importation, evidently borrowed from his reading of the great Russian realists; but it is one which has ultimately no relevance or bearing on the society whose failures and confusions he sets out to expose. The hero's crown of life – the fulfilment of his 'ennobling love' to Irene Derwent, the grand-bourgeois heroine – becomes in the end an image of escape, reminiscent of Gissing's earlier schematic novel, *The Emancipated*. Here, however, the protagonists manifest a more blatant absorption in the world they claim to have transcended. For their triumph depends on successful commerce, whose inevitable inhumanities are exposed but finally glossed over in the hero's Ruskinian ideal. It is a closure which can be seen to mark a final retreat on Gissing's part from the problem of a new, increasingly complex age.

With the exception of the *The Crown of Life*, Gissing's novels after *The Whirlpool* confirm the 'safe prophecy' made by H. G. Wells in 1897. *The Town Traveller, Our Friend the Charlatan, Will Warburton*: the retreat of culture already evident in Rolfe's sardonic resignation to the inevitability of personal and national struggle manifests itself in these last novels in a movement towards impersonality and 'emancipation from the idealising stress'.[8] Written after his critical study of Dickens (1898), these novels can be read as attempts to achieve that critical detachment from, and identity with, contemporary social experience, that combination of externality and representativeness, which Gissing identified as the hallmark of the Dickensian comic mode and the basis of Dickens's popularity and 'realism'.[9] Yet the 'accuracy' of Dickens's work – his ability to make visible the contradictions of the new society, to be both its moral critic and its ideological spokesman – derives, as Gissing argues, from his ambiguous position as a member of the aspiring lower middle class in an age which saw the triumphant rise and expansion of the new liberal society.[10] Though Gissing shares Dickens's social marginality, he belongs, by contrast, to an age in which 'the England that Dickens depicted had hardened into the modern institutionalism of Victorian wealth, smug decorum and industrial success'.[11] The external, indulgent rendering of lower middle-class energy that characterises Gissing's novels after 1897 comes, in this context, to represent a declension from accuracy and representativeness in a world where the optimism of middle-class enterprise and reform has given way to the conditions of struggle and oppression largely created by that historical change. In these conditions, the middle-class definition of the problems of value and identity no longer squares in any representative way with the conditions prevailing in society as a whole. Gissing's indulgence becomes in this context not a distancing device, combining satirical detachment and the 'better dreams of ordinary men'.[12] Rather, it constitutes a moral evasion of that inauthenticity his novels attempt to expose. The renunciation of the favoured hero amounts in effect to a formal and ideological withdrawal from the combative, problematic relationship to society and the reading public which constitutes the veracity and significance of Gissing's work. It indicates a movement to a union of pathos and humour in the portrayal of character which aligns Gissing with those other novelists of the lower classes at the turn of the century, such as Kipling, Bennett and Wells. Yet if Gissing clearly fails in these last works to achieve the combination of representativeness and geniality which he saw to be the principle of Dickens's greatness, he also lacks the incisiveness of his younger contemporaries in confronting the complexities and energies of the modern age. The vigorous naturalism of Bennett and Wells, for instance, is rooted in an imaginative identification with evolutionary progress that marks their commitment to the modern world. It is the basis of their resistance, not only to an idealistic attachment ot the old world, but to the illusions of contemporary escape. In Gissing's last works, by contrast, the seemingly sanguine affirmation of the 'real' remains sardonic.

This supports the present argument that it is in Gissing's continuing commitment to the 'illustrative moral intention' and 'exponential' features of the traditional English novel that the true significance of his work is to be found. In his 'deliberate attempts to present in typical groupings distinct phases of our social order',[13] Gissing clearly belongs within the tradition of post-Flaubertian naturalistic writing. His technique of representation, with its refusal of the resources of the popular comic spirit found in Dickens, is characterised, as we have seen, by a process of immobilisation and abstraction of the social milieu. There is in Gissing's work an acute severance of inner and outer worlds. Character would seem as a result to be average rather than typical, in a specifically Lukácsian sense; that is, it would seem to lack that dialectic unity of the general and the particular, of historical situation and lived human values, which Lukács identified as 'the central category and criterion of realist literature'.[14] Yet the focus of Gissing's work is not in the end a single group or subject circumscribed by a refractory and ineluctable social structure, but the conflict or contradiction of being among the 'unclassed'. This is not the same as *déclassé*, with its possibility of reconciling individual human values with existing society; nor does it refer to a form of consolatory alienation and independence of the social order, generally associated with the isolated artist. Rather, it constitutes the conflicting and irreconcilable desires for autonomy and integration that is the condition of life for those whom society has denied. It corresponds, in social and psychological terms, to the unresolved trauma of the aspiring individual in a world in which man's place in society has become a measure of his social worth, but in which the consequent imperatives of self-validation clash with the rigidities of social, sexual and economic stratification.

In dramatising the conflicting desires of this divided and contradictory consciousness, Gissing's radical critique of conventional society remains tied to the motifs of 'declassing', without being able to effect the reconciliations and settlements that 'resolve' these motifs in the English novel of the classic realist period. Equally, however, there is no final appeal in Gissing's work to the moral centrality of the exilic hero or outsider in the face of an inauthentic world. For though culture may affirm the authority of the inner self, it is located *materially* in the traditions and privileged fellowship of an absent, yet nostalgically reverenced higher social stratum. There is, for this reason, no return in Gissing's 'exponent' novels to that stubborn affirmation of life as it is, which can be seen to characterise, say, the transmutation of H. G. Wells's ironic vision of 'waste' in *Tono Bungay* into an imaginative identification with the reality of human struggle and protest. The effect of Gissing's work is one of disturbing indeterminacy in its simultaneous appeal to, and subversion of humanist idealism. The intention in this context has been to stress not only the nature of Gissing's cultural challenge to the reality of his times, but the continuing cultural challenge of his novels today. The demand has been for a new kind of reader – sceptical, resistant, actively engaged in a reading that confronts the assumptions, paradoxes, silences and ambiguities of the writer's work.

Gissing's novels require such a reader, for their strength and originality, as Virginia Woolf recognised, lies in their capacity to baffle the reader 'whose pleasure it is to identify himself with the hero or heroine'.[15] It is a view which must be taken with her approbation that 'his men and women think'. Virginia Woolf is not simply referring here to Gissing's favoured, intellectual heroes:

Each of the people who for one cause or another has to suffer the worst bruises in the Nether World is a thinking creature, capable not only of feeling, but of making that feeling part of a view of life.[16]

The withdrawal of moral judgement leads in effect to a unique recognition in Gissing's novels that all men are intellectual. Admittedly characters who struggle are satirised for their immersion in a sterile world, particularly in the early tendentious novels; but even here they are also seen to be directed, however delusively, by an inner sense of immunity and refusal of that world, by a commitment to struggle to achieve ultimate autonomy and freedom from the struggles of life. The representatives of both Arnoldian moral aestheticism and liberal individualism display a curious similarity in their claim to exemption from the material conditions on which their lives are seen ultimately to depend. Though Gissing's work is undoubtedly reactionary in its attachment to refined culture, that very adherence is also the basis of a Utopianism that points beyond the inadequacies of both the past and the present to a world that has yet to come into being; that is, in a sense, forever waiting to be born.

The tendency has been to see Gissing's work as a late example of the Victorian tradition of the novel, overladen and enfeebled by elements of pessimism and lower middle-class *malaise*. But Gissing can be seen with more justice as a precursor of that form of naturalistic writing which has retained a strong hold on the English tradition, through Wells, Bennett and Orwell to the present day. Though Wells always wrote of Gissing's work with a kind of youthful condescension, one senses his uneasy awareness that Gissing was more 'artistically adult' than most of his successors.[17] Wells himself was finally to champion an extensive, more open form of the novel, but his own novels about middle-class problems, such as *Ann Veronica*, *Mr Polly* and *Tono Bungay*, were undoubtedly attempts to achieve a kind of seriousness he found in a writer whose work had succeeded so well in exploring the cultural and intellectual currents of contemporary English life at their most hidden and challenging depths.

Notes

Notes to the Introduction

1. P. J. Keating, 'The State of Gissing Studies', *Victorian Studies*, XIII (June 1970) 393.
2. I am indebted for this and other details of Gissing's family background to Clifford Brook, *George Gissing and Wakefield: A Novelist's Association with his Home Town* (Wakefield Historical Publications, 1980).
3. Gillian Tindall, *The Born Exile: George Gissing* (1974) p. 29.
4. Ibid., p. 50.
5. Adrian Poole, *Gissing in Context* (1975) p. 1.
6. Henry Hick, *Henry Hick's Recollections of George Gissing*, ed. Pierre Coustillas (*Enitharmon Gissing Series*, no. 3, 1973) p. 8.
7. *George Gissing's Commonplace Book*, ed. Jacob Korg (1962) p. 29; quoted by Poole, *Gissing in Context*, p. 12.
8. H. G. Wells, 'George Gissing: an Impression', *George Gissing and H. G. Wells: Their Friendship and Correspondence*, ed. R. A. Gettman (1961) p. 261.
9. Thomas Waller Gissing, *Margaret and Other Poems, by An East Anglian* (1855).
10. Thomas Waller Gissing, *The Ferns and Fern Allies of Wakefield and Its Neighbourhood* (Wakefield, 1862), and *Materials for a Flora of Wakefield and Its Neighbourhood* (Huddersfield, 1867).
11. Jacob Korg, *George Gissing: A Critical Biography* (1965) p. 7.
12. Quoted by Brook, *Gissing and Wakefield*, p. 19.
13. See J. R. McKim, 'Reminiscences of an Old Master', *George Gissing at Alderley Edge*, ed. Pierre Coustillas (1969) p. 9.
14. See Sheldon Rothblatt, *Tradition and Change in English Liberal Education: An Essay in History and Culture* (1976).
15. McKim, 'Reminiscences', p. 10.
16. Rothblatt, *Tradition and Change*, p. 133.
17. Ibid., p. 134.
18. George Gissing, 'The Old School', *George Gissing at Alderley Edge*, pp. 30–1.

19. See especially Matthew Arnold, *Culture and Anarchy: The Complete Prose Works of Matthew Arnold*, ed. R. H. Super, vol. V (1965).
20. See Joseph Thompson, *The Owen's College: Its Foundation and Growth and its Connection with Victoria University, Manchester* (1886).
21. Ibid., p. 135.
22. Brian Simon, *Studies in the History of Education, 1780–1870* (1960).
23. Ibid., p. 282.
24. Matthew Arnold, 'The Function of Criticism at the Present Time', *The Complete Prose Works*, vol. III, pp. 258–85.
25. Raymond Williams, *Culture and Society, 1780–1950* (1958) p. 127.
26. Margaret Mathieson, *The Preachers of Culture: A Study of English and its Teachers* (1975) pp. 42–3.
27. The historical arguments supporting this view are put forward by Simon, *History of Education*. For a more 'factual' and essentially 'unsociological' account of state intervention in education, see David Wardle, *The Rise of the Schooled Society: The History of Formal Schooling in England* (1974).
28. H. G. Wells, *Experiment in Autobiography*, vol. II (1934) p. 570.
29. Rothblatt, *Tradition and Change*, p. 124.
30. See Melvin Richter, *The Politics of Conscience: T. H. Green and his Age* (1964) p. 355.
31. T. H. Green, 'The Grading of Secondary Schools', *Works*, vol. III (1888) p. 403.
32. Letter to Algernon, 22 September 1886, in *The Letters of George Gissing to Members of his Family*, ed. Algernon and Ellen Gissing (1927) p. 184; hereafter cited as *Letters*.
33. Thomas Carlyle, 'Shooting Niagara: and After?', *Critical and Miscellaneous Essays*, vol. V (Centenary Edition, *The Works of Thomas Carlyle*, (1899) p. 24.
34. Korg, *George Gissing*, p. 70.
35. Letter to Morley Roberts, 10 February 1895; quoted by Morley Roberts, *The Private Life of Henry Maitland* (1912) p. 311.
36. Gabrielle Fleury to H. G. Wells, June 1901; *George Gissing and H. G. Wells*, p. 169.
37. Simon, *History of Education*, p. 335.
38. Wells, *Experiment in Autobiography*.
39. Ibid., pp. 570–1.
40. H. G. Wells, 'The Novels of Mr George Gissing', *Contemporary Review*, vol. LXXII (August 1897) 192–201; reprinted in *Gissing: The Critical Heritage*, ed. Pierre Coutillas and Colin Partridge (1972) pp. 296–305; hereafter abbreviated to *CH*.
41. Frederic Jameson, *The Political Unconscious: Narrative as a Socially Symbolic Art* (1981) p. 152.
42. Williams, *Culture and Society*, p. 178.
43. Frank Swinnerton, *George Gissing: A Critical Study* (1912) p. 14.
44. Virginia Woolf, 'The Novels of George Gissing', *TLS*, 11 January 1912, 9–10; reprinted in *CH*, pp. 529–534.
45. Henry James, 'London Notes', *Harper's Weekly*, 31 July 1897, 754; reprinted in *CH*, pp. 290–4.

46. Ibid., p. 290.
47. Henry James, 'The Younger Generation', *Henry James and H. G. Wells: A Record of their Friendship, their Debate on the Art of Fiction, and their Quarrel*, ed. Leon Edel and Gordon N. Ray (1958) p. 185.
48. James, 'London Notes', p. 290.

Notes to Chapter 1   Hogarthian Beginnings

1. Poole, *Gissing in Context*.
2. Ibid., p. 8.
3. Arnold Kettle, *An Introduction to the English Novel*, vol. II: *Henry James to the Present Day* (1967, second edn) pp. 97–8.
4. Eduard Bertz, 'George Gissing: ein Real-Idealist', *Deutsche Press*, November 1889; reprinted in translation in *CH*, pp. 149–56.
5. Mario Praz, *The Hero in Eclipse in Victorian Fiction* (1956) p. 13.
6. John Harvey, *Victorian Novelists and their Illustrators* (1970).
7. Charles Dickens, 'Preface' to *Oliver Twist* (the Clarendon Dickens, 1966) p. lxiv.
8. George Gissing, *Charles Dickens: A Critical Study* (1898) pp. 31–2.
9. John Goode, *George Gissing: Ideology and Fiction* (1978).
10. Letter to Algernon, 3 November 1880, in *Letters*, p. 83.
11. Goode, *Gissing: Ideology and Fiction*, p. 53.
12. Georg Lukács, *The Theory of the Novel*, trans. Anna Bostock (Merlin Press, 1971; first published in Berlin, 1920).
13. Poole, *Gissing in Context*, p. 61.
14. One might recall, for instance, W. R. Greg's attack on Elizabeth Gaskell – see *Edinburgh Review*, LXXXIX (April 1849).
15. See Gareth Stedman-Jones, *Outcast London: A Study in the Relationship between Classes in Victorian England* (1971).
16. 'Notes on Social Democracy', *Pall Mall Gazette*, 9, 11 and 14 September 1880; reprinted in *Enitharmon Gissing Series*, no. 1 (1968).
17. Brian Simon, *Education and the Labour Movement 1870–1920* (1965).
18. 'Notes on Social Democracy', p. 13.
19. Letter to Algernon, 2 January 1880, in *Letters*, p. 53.
20. Werner Picht, *Toynbee Hall and the English Settlement Movement*, trans. L. A. Cowell (1914).
21. Richter, *Politics of Conscience*, p. 167.
22. See George Gissing, 'The Hope of Pessimism' (1882), in *George Gissing: Essays and Fiction*, ed. Pierre Coustillas (1970) pp. 75–97.
23. Edith Sichel, 'Two Philanthropic Novelists: Mr Walter Besant and Mr George Gissing', *Murray's Magazine* (April 1888); reprinted in *CH*, pp. 114–26.
24. See especially Georg Lukács, *The Historical Novel*, trans. Hannah and Stanley Mitchell (1962).
25. Victor Brombert, *The Intellectual Hero: Studies in the French Novel 1880–1955* (1960) pp. 38–9.
26. Quoted by W. McG. Eager, *Making Men: The History of Boys' Clubs and Related Movements in Great Britain* (1953) p. 202.

27. Edward Shils, *The Intellectuals and the Powers, and Other Essays* (Chicago, 1972) p. 148.
28. Antonio Gramsci, 'The Formation of Intellectuals', *Selections from the Prison Notebooks*, ed. Quintin Hoare and Geoffrey Nowell Smith (1971).
29. Williams, *Culture and Society*, pp. 179–85.
30. For this notion of a rupture between authentic search and fictional degradation, see Lukács, *The Theory of the Novel*.
31. Raymond Williams, *The Country and the City* (1973) p. 176.
32. Karl Mannheim, *Essays in the Sociology of Culture* (1956) p. 150.

Notes to Chapter 2 Residues of Romance

1. George Meredith acted as manuscript reader for Chapman and Hall who published both *The Unclassed* and *Isabel Clarendon*. 'Meredith tells me I am making a great mistake in leaving the low-life scenes', Gissing wrote to his brother about *Isabel Clarendon*, 'says I might take a foremost place in fiction if I pursued that.' Letter to Algernon, 31 October 1885, in *Letters*, p. 172.
2. See especially Goode, 'The Evolution of the Gissing Novel', in *Gissing: Ideology and Fiction*, pp. 71–108.
3. See especially letter to Algernon, 18 July 1883, in *Letters*, pp. 128–9.
4. 'The Hope of Pessimism'.
5. 'Preface' to *The Unclassed* (1895).
6. Terry Eagleton, *Exiles and Emigrés: Studies in Modern Literature* (1970) p. 14.
7. A point made by Poole, *Gissing in Context*, p. 66.
8. Ian Watt, *The Rise of the Novel: Studies in Defoe, Richardson and Fielding* (1957) p. 154.
9. Ibid., p. 9.
10. James Ashcroft Noble, *Academy*, XXX (10 July 1886) 24; reprinted in *CH*, pp. 96–7.
11. See Lukács, *The Theory of the Novel*.
12. Goode, *Gissing: Ideology and Fiction*, p. 83.
13. Morley Roberts, *The Private Life of Henry Maitland* (1912) p. 167.
14. For a brief survey of critics who have taken this approach, see Pierre Coustillas, 'Introduction' to *Isabel Clarendon* (Brighton, 1969) pp. xlix–l.
15. Williams, *Culture and Society*.
16. Williams, *The Country and the City*, p. 36.
17. See E. Lynn Linton, *The Girl of the Period, and Other Social Essays*, 2 vols (1883).
18. See especially Sigmund Freud, 'Femininity', in *The Standard Edition of the Complete Psychological Works of Sigmund Freud*, trans. under the general editorship of J. Stanley (1953–74); vol. XXII, pp. 112–35.
19. For an account of feminist theory, see Jonathan Culler, *On Deconstruction: Theory and Criticism after Structuralism* (1983) pp. 165–75.
20. Letter to Ellen, 2 August 1885, in *Letters*, p. 160.
21. Gabriel Josipovici, *The World and the Book: A Study of Modern Fiction* (1979; second edn) pp. 123–4.

22. Goode, *Gissing: Ideology and Fiction*, p. 84.
23. Unsigned review, *Guardian* (London), 23 January 1889, xliv (I), 136; reprinted in *CH*, p. 131.
24. Korg, *George Gissing*, p. 81.
25. See Sigmund Freud, 'The Economic Problem of Masochism', *Standard Edition*, vol. XIX, pp. 159–70.
26. Ibid, p. 170.

Notes to Chapter 3   Gissing and 'The People'

1. Unsigned review, *Athenaeum*, 10 April 1886, 485; reprinted in *CH*, p. 81.
2. For an outline of these traditions, see P. J. Keating, *The Working Classes in Victorian Fiction* (1971) pp. 54–5.
3. Ibid., pp. 227–8.
4. John Lucas, 'Dickens and *Dombey and Son*: Past and Present Imperfect', *Tradition and Tolerance in Nineteenth-Century Fiction*, ed. D. Howard, J. Lucas and J. Goode (1966) pp. 99–140.
5. Sichel, 'Two Philanthropic Novelists'.
6. See Stedman-Jones, *Outcast London*.
7. Williams, *Culture and Society*, p. 178.
8. Letter to Algernon, 31 October 1885, in *Letters*, p. 172.
9. John Goode, 'The Nether World', *Tradition and Tolerance in Nineteenth-Century Fiction*, pp. 207–9.
10. Williams, *Culture and Society*, pp. 175–9.
11. Derek Jarrett, *England in the Age of Hogarth* (1974) p. 99.
12. John Goode, 'Gissing, Morris, and English Socialism', *Victorian Studies*, XII (December 1968) 206–26.
13. Matthew Arnold, 'The Study of Poetry', *The Complete Prose Works*, vol. IX, p. 161.
14. As John Lucas suggests in 'Conservatism and Revolution in the 1880s', *Literature and Politics in the Nineteenth Century*, ed. John Lucas (1971) pp. 211–12; his modified view of this restoration as 'less a gesture of hope than of despair' is nearer the truth (ibid., p. 214).
15. Unsigned review, New York *Daily Tribune*, 9 May 1886, 10; reprinted in *CH*, pp. 90–1.
16. Unsigned review, *Guardian* (London), 14 April 1886, xli (1), 554; reprinted in *CH*, pp. 86–8.
17. Letter to Margaret, 31 July 1886, in *Letters*, p. 182.
18. Arnold, *Culture and Anarchy*, p. 95.
19. Poole, *Gissing in Context*, p. 82.
20. Ibid., p. 78.
21. Sichel, 'Two Philanthropic Novelists', *CH*, p. 18.
22. Letter to Ellen, 16 January 1887, in *Letters*, p. 189.
23. Entry, 1 March 1888; *London and the Life of Literature in Late Victorian England: The Diary of George Gissing*, ed. Pierre Coustillas (1978) p. 23; hereafter referred to as *Diary*.

24. Frederick W. Farrar, review in *Contemporary Review*, September 1889, lvi, 370–80; reprinted in *CH*, pp. 141–6.
25. Frederic Jameson, 'Authentic Ressentiment: the "Experimental" Novels of Gissing', *Nineteenth Century Fiction* (September 1976) 127–49.
26. Samuel V. Gapp, *George Gissing: Classicist* (1936) p. 160.

Notes to Chapter 4   The Measure of Success

1. See Korg, *George Gissing*, pp. 121–2.
2. *Diary*, 19 October 1888, p. 54.
3. Ibid., 13 June 1888, p. 32.
4. Ibid., 1 March 1888, p. 23.
5. For an account of Gissing's trip to Italy, see ibid., 29 October 1888 to 26 February 1889, pp. 59–141.
6. Korg, *George Gissing*, p. 136.
7. Roland Barthes, 'The Writer on Holiday', *Mythologies* (1973; first published in France, 1957) pp. 29–31.
8. Marilyn Butler, *Romantics, Rebels and Reactionaries: English Literature and its Background, 1760–1830* (1981) p. 72.
9. Korg, *George Gissing*, p. 154.
10. Bernard Bergonzi, 'Introduction' to *New Grub Street* (1968) p. 9.
11. Letter to *Pall Mall Gazette*, 15 December 1884, 2.
12. Letter to Clodd, 1 September 1898, in *Letters of George Gissing to Edward Clodd*, ed. Pierre Coustillas (*Enitharmon Gissing Series*, no. 7, 1973) p. 51.
13. Q. D. Leavis, 'Gissing and the English Novel', *Scrutiny*, VII (June 1938) 73–81.
14. Ibid., p. 76.
15. Poole, pp. 144–6.
16. For a discussion of literature's 'determinate freedom', see Pierre Macherey, *A Theory of Literary Production*, trans. Geoffrey Wall (1978; first published in Paris, 1966).
17. Letter to Bertz, 26 April 1891, in *The Letters of George Gissing to Edward Bertz, 1887–1903*, ed. Arthur C. Young (1961) p. 122; hereafter referred to as *LEB*.
18. Butler, *Romantics, Rebels and Reactionaries*, p. 74.
19. Wells, *Experiment in Autobiography*, p. 527.
20. Poole, *Gissing in Context*, p. 152.
21. For a discussion of death-bed scenes, see Margaret Holubetz, 'Death-Bed Scenes in Victorian Fiction', *English Studies*, 67 (I) (February 1986) 14–34.
22. Walter Benjamin, 'The Author as Producer', *New Left Review*, 62 (1970) 83–96.
23. Eagleton, *Exiles and Emigrés*.
24. Goode, *Gissing: Ideology and Fiction*, p. 117.
25. See Michael Collie, *The Alien Art: A Critical Study of George Gissing's Novels* (1979) p. 126. Collie tries to give an objective basis to his belief that the novel is 'not about publishing' but about marriage in his account of Gissing's revision for the French

edition of *New Grub Street*, in 'Gissing's Revision of *New Grub Street*', *The Yearbook of English Studies*, IV (1974) 212–24.
26. Goode, *Gissing: Ideology and Fiction*, p. 136.

Notes to Chapter 5   The Refusal of Irony

1. Walter Allen, 'Introduction' to *Born in Exile* (1970) p. 5.
2. Jacob Korg, 'The Spiritual Theme in *Born in Exile*, in *From Jane Austen to Joseph Conrad*, ed. Robert C. Rathburn and Martin Steinmann (1958) pp. 246–56.
3. Pierre Coustillas, 'Introduction' to *Born in Exile* (1978) p. xx.
4. Swinnerton, *Gissing: Critical Study*, p. 103.
5. Goode, *Gissing: Ideology and Fiction*, p. 67.
6. Coustillas, 'Introduction' to *Born in Exile*, p. xx.
7. For a discussion of the 'typicality' of Dickens's characters, see Goode, *Gissing: Ideology and Fiction*, pp. 28–33.
8. Sigmund Freud, 'Taboo and Emotional Ambivalence', *Standard Edition*, vol. XIII, p. 49.
9. Poole, *Gissing in Context*, p. 168.
10. Nicholas Berdyaev, *Dostoevsky: An Interpretation*, trans. Donald Attwater (1934) p. 135.

Notes to Chapter 6   Oddness and Typicality

1. Letter to Bertz, 16 February 1892, in *LEB*, p. 144.
2. Lloyd Fernando, *'New Women' in the Late Victorian Novel* (1977).
3. Letter to Bertz, 17 March 1892, in *LEB*, p. 150.
4. Letter to Bertz, 1 May 1892, in *LEB*, p. 151.
5. Letter to Bertz, 19 June 1892, in *LEB*, p. 157.
6. 'The writing has been as severe a struggle as ever I knew', Gissing wrote. 'Not an hour when I was really at peace in mind. A bitter struggle' (*Diary*, 4 October 1892, p. 286).
7. Ibid., 1 July 1892, p. 280.
8. Letter to Bertz, 7 August 1892, in *LEB*, p. 158.
9. *Diary*, 6 August 1892, p. 283.
10. Ibid., 5 August 1892, p. 283.
11. Letter to Bertz, 30 August 1892, in *LEB*, p. 160.
12. Letter to Bertz, 2 June 1893, in *LEB*, p. 172.
13. Korg, *George Gissing*, p. 190.
14. John Goode, 'The Art of Fiction: Walter Besant and Henry James', *Tradition and Tolerance in Nineteenth-Century Fiction* (1966) 243–81.
15. Ibid., p. 275.
16. See Harriet Martineau, 'Female Industry', *Edinburgh Review*, CCXXII (April 1859).
17. See W. R. Greg, 'Why are Women Redundant?', *National Review*, XIV (April 1862) 434–60.

18. Alison Cotes, 'New Women and Odd Women', *Gissing Newsletter*, XIV (April 1978) 1–20.
19. There is evidence that the practice of placing women in clerical positions formerly monopolised by men was already successfully established by the 1870s. See evidence of Gertrude King to the (Playfair) Civil Service Inquiry Commission (1874); quoted in Patricia Hollis, *Women in Public 1850–1900: Documents of the Victorian Women's Movement* (1979) pp. 104–5.
20. See John Ruskin, 'Of Queen's Gardens', *Sesame and Lilies* (1865); for the influence of this ideal on the English novel, see Patricia Thomson, *The Victorian Heroine: A Changing Ideal 1837–73* (1956).
21. See Gail Cunningham, *The New Woman and the Victorian Novel* (1978).
22. Lynn Linton, 'Modern Man-Haters', *The Girl of the Period*, vol. II, pp. 173–60.
23. Ibid., p. 179.
24. Gissing was subsequently to become a friend of Clara Collet who was an advocate not only of the usefulness of 'permanent spinsters', but of the need for single women to form a 'compact band' to give unity to the management of their associations; Collet's views are quoted in Hollis, *Women in Public*, p. 170. Gissing's friendship with Clara Collet is discussed by Ruth M. Adams, 'George Gissing and Clara Collet', *Nineteenth-Century Fiction*, XI (June 1956) 72–7.
25. Kate Millett, *Sexual Politics* (1971) p. 116.
26. As Millett recognises: 'chastity, or even the negative attitudes towards coitus which accompany frigidity . . . could also be transformed into protective feminine "stratagems" in a refusal to capitulate to patriarchal force; physical, or social' (ibid., p. 116).
27. Goode, *Gissing: Ideology and Fiction*, p. 145.
28. Watt, *Rise of the Novel*, pp. 139–40.
29. Fernando, 'New Women', p. 120.
30. Margaret Walters, 'Introduction' to *The Odd Women* (1980).

Notes to Chapter 7   Towards the Vortex

1. H. G. Wells, 'The Novels of Mr George Gissing', pp. 299–302.
2. Ibid., p. 304.
3. Letter to Wells, 7 August 1897, in Gettman, *Gissing and Wells*, p. 48.
4. Ibid., p. 48.
5. Wells, 'The Novels of Mr George Gissing', p. 302.
6. Ibid., pp. 296–7.
7. See Fernando, 'New Women'.
8. Ibid., p. 121.
9. *Diary*, 22 April 1893, p. 302.
10. Letter to Bertz, 1 May 1892, in *LEB*, p. 151.
11. Williams, *The Country and the City*, pp. 233–9.
12. See Poole, *Gissing in Context*, p. 42.
13. Swinnerton, *Gissing: Critical Study*, p. 185.

14. Wells, *Experiment in Autobiography*, pp. 571–2.
15. Poole, *Gissing in Context*, p. 50.
16. Goode, *Gissing: Ideology and Fiction*, p. 164.
17. Gillian Tindall, 'Introduction' to *In the Year of Jubilee* (1976) p. xvi.
18. Robert L. Selig, 'A Sad Heart at the Late-Victorian Culture Market: George Gissing's *In the Year of Jubilee*', *Studies in English Literature, 1500–1900* (Autumn 1969) 703–20.
19. Françoise Basch, *Relative Creatures: Victorian Women in Society and the Novel 1837–67*, trans. Anthony Rudolf (1974) p. 246.
20. Ibid., p. 261.
21. Poole, *Gissing in Context*, p. 197.
22. Goode, *Gissing: Ideology and Fiction*, p. 176.
23. Tindall, 'Introduction' to *In the Year of Jubilee*, p. xvi.
24. Carol Dyhouse, 'The Role of Women: from Self-Sacrifice to Self-Awareness', *The Victorians*, ed. Laurence Lerner (1978) p. 189.
25. David Thomson, *England in the Nineteenth Century, 1815–1914* (1978) p. 172.
26. E. J. Hobsbawm, *Industry and Empire* (1968) p. 141.
27. Ibid., p. 142.
28. Eagleton, *Exiles and Emigrés*, p. 73.
29. Patrick Parrinder, 'Introduction' to *The Whirlpool* (1977) p. xvi.
30. Quoted by F. W. J. Hemmings, 'The Realist and the Naturalist Movement in France', *The Age of Realism* (1974) p. 159.
31. Williams, *The Country and the City*, p. 227.
32. Henry James, *The Art of the Novel*, ed. Richard P. Blackmur (1934) p. 145.
33. Ibid., p. 142.
34. Letter to Bullen, 8 February 1877; quoted in Colin Partridge, 'The Humane Centre: George Gissing's *The Whirlpool*', *Gissing Newsletter*, IX (July 1973) 1–10.

Notes to the Conclusion

1. Arnold Bennett, 'Mr George Gissing, an Inquiry', in *CH*, p. 362.
2. C. F. G. Masterman, 'George Gissing', in *CH*, pp. 491–2.
3. Letter to Stanislaus Joyce, 20 November 1906, in *The Letters of James Joyce*, vol. II, ed. Richard Ellman (1966) p. 196.
4. Eagleton, *Exiles and Emigrés*, p. 73.
5. See Guinevere L. Griest, *Mudie's Circulating Library and the Victorian Novel* (1971).
6. Quoted by Austin Harrison, 'George Gissing', *Nineteenth-Century and After*, LX (September 1906) 463.
7. Williams, *The Country and the City*, p. 245.
8. Wells, 'The Novels of Mr George Gissing', p. 301.
9. Gissing, *Charles Dickens: A Critical Study* (1898).
10. Ibid., p. 8.
11. Austin Harrison, quoted by W. C. Frierson, *The English Novel in Transition, 1885–1940* (1965) p. 101.

12. Gissing's description of Dickens's work in *Charles Dickens: A Critical Study*, p. 83.
13. Wells, 'The Novels of Mr George Gissing', p. 297.
14. Georg Lukács, *Studies in European Realism*, trans. Edith Bone (1950).
15. Woolf, 'The Novels of George Gissing', p. 523.
16. Ibid., pp. 523–4.
17. Letter from H. G. Wells to Arnold Bennett, 9 September 1902 in, *Arnold Bennett and H. G. Wells: A Record of a Personal and a Literary Friendship*, ed. Harris Wilson (1960) p. 85.

Select Bibliography

The date of first publication is given and, if applicable, the publisher and date of the modern edition to which references in the text refer.

Workers in the Dawn (1880; Brighton: Harvester Press, 1985).

The Unclassed (1884; revised edn, 1895; Hassocks: Harvester Press, 1972).

Demos: A Story of English Socialism (1886; Hassocks: Harvester Press, 1972).

Isabel Clarendon (1886; Hassocks: Harvester Press, 1972).

Thyrza: A Tale (1887; Hassocks: Harvester Press, 1974).

A Life's Morning (1888; Brighton: Harvester Press, 1984).

The Nether World (1889; Brighton: Harvester Press, 1984).

The Emancipated (1890; Brighton: Harvester Press, 1977).

New Grub Street (1891; 3 vols, London: Smith, Elder and Co., 1891).

Denzil Quarrier (1892; Hassocks: Harvester Press, 1977).

Born in Exile (1892; Hassocks: Harvester Press, 1978).

The Odd Women (1893; London: Anthony Blond, 1968).

In the Year of Jubilee (1894; Hassocks: Harvester Press, 1976).

Eve's Ranson (1895; New York: Dover, 1981).

The Paying Guest (1895; Brighton: Harvester Press, 1982).

Sleeping Fires (1895; Hassocks: Harvester Press, 1974).

The Whirlpool (1897; Hassocks: Harvester Press, 1977).

Human Odds and Ends: Stories and Sketches (1898; London: Lawrence and Bullen, 1898).

The Town Traveller (1898; Hassocks: Harvester Press, 1978).

The Crown of Life (1899; Hassocks: Harvester Press, 1978).

Our Friend the Charlatan (1901; Hassocks: Harvester Press, 1976).

The Private Papers of Henry Ryecroft (1903; Brighton: Harvester Press, 1982).

Veranilda: A Romance (1904; Brighton: Harvester Press, 1987).

Will Warburton: A Romance of Real Life (1905; Brighton: Harvester Press, 1981).

The House of Cobwebs, and Other Stories (1906; London: Archibald Constable, 1906).

The Sins of the Father, and Other Tales (1924; Chicago: Pascal Corici, 1924).

A Victim of Circumstances, and Other Stories (1927; London: Constable, 1927).

Brownie (1931; New York: Columbia University Press, 1931).

Stories and Sketches (1938; London: Michael Joseph, 1938).

My First Rehearsal and my Clerical Revival (1970; London: Enitharmon Press, 1970).

George Gissing: Essays and Fiction (Baltimore and London: Johns Hopkins Press, 1970).

NON-FICTION

For a check-list of Gissing's writings on Dickens, see Pierre Coustillas (ed.), *Gissing's Writings on Dickens: A Bio-bibliographical Survey* (London: Enitharmon Press, 1969); and for his writings on fiction, see Jacob and Cynthia Korg (eds), *George Gissing on Fiction* (London: Enitharmon Press, 1978).

'Notes of Social Democracy', *Pall Mall Gazette*, 9, 11 and 14 September 1880; reprinted by Enitharmon Press, 1968.

'Why I Don't Write Plays', *Pall Mall Gazette*, 10 September 1892.

'The Place of Realism in Fiction', in *Selections Autobiographical and Imaginative from the Works of George Gissing*, ed. Alfred C. Gissing (London: Jonathan Cape, 1929).

Charles Dickens: A Critical Study (London: Blackie and Son, 1898).

'The Coming of the Preacher', *Literature*, 6 January 1900, 15–16.

By the Ionian Sea: Notes of a Ramble in Southern Italy (London: Chapman and Hall, 1901).

'Dickens in Memory', *Literature*, 2 December 1901.

The Immortal Dickens (London: Cecil Palmer, 1924).

George Gissing's Commonplace Book, ed. Jacob Korg (New York: New York Public Library, 1962).

'The Hope of Pessimism' (1882, unpublished), in *George Gissing: Essays and Fiction*, ed. Pierre Coustillas (Baltimore and London: Johns Hopkins Press, 1970).

London and the Life of Literature in Late Victorian England: The Diary of George Gissing, ed. Pierre Coustillas (Hassocks: Harvester Press, 1978).

LETTERS

Letter to Morley Roberts, 10 February 1895; published in *The Bookman*, XLVII, January 1915, and reprinted in *Gissing: The Critical Heritage*, ed. Pierre Coustillas and Colin Partridge (London and Boston: Routledge and Kegan Paul, 1972); hereafter referred to by its title.

The Letters of George Gissing to Members of His Family, ed. Algernon and Ellen Gissing (London: Constable, 1927).

The Letters of George Gissing to Eduard Bertz, ed. A. C. Young (London: Constable, 1961).

George Gissing and H. G. Wells: A Record of Their Friendship and Correspondence, ed. Royal A. Gettmann (London: Rupert Hart-Davis, 1961).

The Letters of George Gissing to Gabrielle Fleury, ed. Pierre Coustillas (New York: New York Public Library, 1964).

Six letters to Thomas Hardy, in Pierre Coustillas, 'Some Unpublished Letters from Gissing to Hardy', *English Literature in Transition*, IX, 4 (1966) 197–209.

Fifty-four letters, in *Henry Hick's Recollections of George Gissing*, ed. Pierre Coustillas (London: Enitharmon Press, 1973).

The Letters of George Gissing to Edward Clodd, ed. Pierre Coustillas (London: Enitharmon Press, 1973).

Landscapes and Literati: Unpublished Letters of W. H. Hudson and George Gissing, ed. Dennis Shrubsall and Pierre Coustillas (Wilton: Michael Russell, 1985).

WRITINGS ABOUT GISSING: SELECTED BIOGRAPHY AND CRITICISM

A useful bibliographical guide to early research is *Victorian Fiction: A Guide to Research*, ed. Lionel Stevenson (Harvard:

Modern Language Association of America, 1964). Information about more recent research is to be found in *George Gissing: An Annotated Bibliography of Writings about Him*, compiled by Joseph J. Wolff (Dekalb, Ill.: Northern Illinois University Press, 1974); and *Victorian Fiction: A Second Guide to Research*, ed. George H. Ford (New York: Modern Language Association of America, 1978).

Adams, Ruth M., 'George Gissing and Clara Collet', *Nineteenth Century Fiction*, XI (June 1956) 72–7.

Bennett, Arnold, 'Mr George Gissing: an Inquiry', *Academy*, lvii (16 December 1899) 724–6; reprinted in *Gissing: The Critical Heritage*, pp. 361–5.

Brook, Clifford, *George Gissing and Wakefield: A Novelist's Association with his Home Town* (Wakefield: Wakefield Historical Publications, 1980).

Collie, Michael, *George Gissing: A Biography* (Folkstone: Dawson, 1977).

Collie, Michael, *The Alien Art: A Critical Study of George Gissing's Novels* (Folkstone: Dawson, 1979).

Coustillas, Pierre, 'George Gissing et H. G. Wells', *Etudes Anglaises* (April–June 1962) 156–66.

Coustillas, Pierre, 'George Gissing à Manchester', *Etudes Anglaises* (July–September 1963) 254–61.

Coustillas, Pierre, *George Gissing at Alderley Edge* (London: Enitharmon Press, 1970).

Coustillas, Pierre (ed.), *Collected Articles on George Gissing* (London: Cass, 1968).

Coustillas, Pierre and Partridge, Colin (eds), *Gissing: The Critical Heritage* (London and Boston: Routledge and Kegan Paul, 1972).

Donnelly, Mabel C., *George Gissing: Grave Comedian* (Cambridge, Mass.: Harvard University Press, 1954).

Gapp, Samuel V., *George Gissing, Classicist* (Philadelphia: University of Pennsylvania Press, 1936).

Gettmann, Royal A., 'Bentley and Gissing', *Nineteenth Century Fiction*, XI (March 1957) 306–14.

Gissing, Alfred C., 'George Gissing – Some Aspects of His Life and Work', *National Review*, XCIII (August 1929) 932–41.

Gissing, Alfred C., 'Gissing's Unfinished Romance', *National Review*, CVII (January 1937) 82–91.

Gissing, Ellen, 'George Gissing: a Character Sketch', *Nineteenth Century and After*, CII (September 1927) 417–24.

Gissing, Ellen, 'Some Personal Recollections of George Gissing', *Blackwood's Magazine*, CCXXV (May 1929) 653–60.

Gissing Newsletter, vols I– (January 1965–).

Goode, John, 'George Gissing's *The Nether World*', *Tradition and Tolerance in Nineteenth-Century Fiction*, by David Howard, John Lucas and John Goode (London: Routledge and Kegan Paul, 1966) pp. 207–41.

Goode, John, 'Gissing, Morris, and English Socialism', *Victorian Studies*, XII, 2 (December 1968) 201–26.

Goode, John, *George Gissing: Ideology and Fiction* (London: Vision Press, 1978).

Grylls, David, *The Paradox of Gissing* (Hemel Hempstead: Allen and Unwin, 1986).

Halperin, John, *Gissing: A Life in Books* (Oxford: Oxford University Press, 1982).

Harrison, Austin, 'George Gissing', *Nineteenth Century and After*, LX (September 1906) 453–63.

James, Henry, 'London Notes', *Harper's Weekly*, 31 July 1897, 754; reprinted in *Gissing: The Critical Heritage*, pp. 290–4.

Jameson, Frederic, 'Authentic Ressentiment: the Experimental Novels of Gissing', *Nineteenth-Century Fiction* (September 1976) 127–141.

Keating, P. J., *George Gissing: New Grub Street* (Studies in English Literature, no. 33) (London: Edward Arnold, 1968).

Keating, P. J., 'The State of Gissing Studies', *Victorian Studies*, XIII, 4 (June 1970) 394–6.

Keating, P. J., *The Working Classes in Victorian Fiction* (London: Routledge and Kegan Paul, 1971).

Kirk, Russell, 'Who Knows George Gissing?', *Western Humanities Review*, IV (Summer 1950) 213–22.

Koike, Shigeru; Kamo, Güchi; Coustillas, Pierre and Kohler, C. C., *Gissing East and West* (London: Enitharmon Press, 1970).

Korg, Jacob, 'Division of Purpose in George Gissing', *PMLA*, LXX (June 1955) 323–6.

Korg, Jacob, 'The Spiritual Theme of Born in Exile', in *From Jane Austen to Joseph Conrad*, ed. Robert C. Rathburn and Martin Steinmann (Minneapolis; University of Minnesota Press, 1958).

Korg, Jacob, *George Gissing: A Critical Biography* (London: Methuen, 1965).

Leavis, Q. D., 'Gissing and the English Novel', *Scrutiny*, VII (June 1938) 73–81.

Lelchuk, Alan, '*Demos*: the Ordeal of the Two Gissings', *Victorian Studies*, XII, 3 (March 1969) 357–74.

McKay, Ruth C., *George Gissing and his Critic Frank Swinnerton* (Philadelphia: University of Pennyslvania, 1933).

Michaux, Jean-Pierre (ed.), *Critical Essays: George Gissing* (London: Vision Press, 1981).

Poole, Adrian, *Gissing in Context* (London: Macmillan, 1975).

Purdy, R. L., 'George Gissing at Max Gate', *Yale University Library Gazette*, XVII, 3 (January 1943) 51–2.

Roberts, Morley, *The Private Life of Henry Maitland* (London: Nash, Eveleigh, 1912).

Seccombe, Thomas, 'Introduction' to *The House of Cobwebs* (1906).

Selig, Robert L., 'A Sad heart at the Late Victorian Culture Market', *Studies in English Literature 1500–1900*, IX, 4 (Autumn 1969) 703–20.

Selig, Robert L., 'The Valley of the Shadow of Books: Alienation in Gissing's *New Grub Street*', *Nineteenth Century Fiction*, XXV, 2 (September 1970) 188–98.

Sichel, Edith, 'Two Philanthropic Novelists: Mr Walter Besant and Mr George Gissing', *Murray's Magazine*, (April 1888) 506–18; reprinted in *Gissing: The Critical Heritage*, pp. 114–26.

Spiers, John and Coustillas, Pierre, *The Rediscovery of George Gissing: A Reader's Guide to the National Book League Gissing Exhibition* (London: National Book League, 1971).

Swinnerton, Frank, *George Gissing: A Critical Study* (London: Martin Secker, 1912).

Thomas, J. D., 'The Public Purposes of George Gissing', *Nineteenth-Century Fiction*, VIII (September 1953) 118–23.

Tindall, Gillian, *The Born Exile: George Gissing* (London: Temple Smith, 1974).

Wells, H. G., 'The Novels of Mr George Gissing', *Contemporary Review*, LXXII (August 1897) 192–201; reprinted in *Gissing: The Critical Heritage*, pp. 295–305.

Wells, H. G., 'George Gissing: an Impression', *Monthly Review*, XVI (August 1904) 160–72.

Wells, H. G., *Experiment in Autobiography: Discoveries and Conclusions of a Very Ordinary Brain (since 1866)*, vol. II, pp. 567–81 (London: Gollancz, 1934).

Wolff, Joseph J., 'Gissing's Revision of *The Unclassed*', *Nineteenth-Century Fiction*, VIII (June 1953) 45–52.

Woolf, Virginia, 'The Novels of George Gissing', *TLS*, 11 January 1912, 9–10; reprinted in *Gissing: The Critical Heritage*, pp. 529–34.

Woolf, Virginia, 'George Gissing', *Collected Essays*, vol. 2, pp. 297–301 (London: Hogarth Press, 1966). Originally published in *The Common Reader*, Second Series (London: Hogarth Press, 1932).

Yates, May, *George Gissing: An Appreciation* (Manchester: University Press, 1922).

Young, A. C., 'George Gissing's Friendship with Eduard Bertz', *Nineteenth Century Fiction*, XIII (December 1958) 227–37.

Index

DATE DUE

MAR 2 2 1997	